# LET THEM CHOOSE

## CHOOSE

Cafeteria Learning Style for Adults

Jillian Douglas and Shannon McKenzie

PRESS

19  18  17  16          1  2  3  4  5

ATD Press is an internationally renowned source of insightful and practical information on
talent development, workplace learning, and professional development.

**ATD Press**
1640 King Street
Alexandria, VA 22314 USA

Ordering information: Books published by ATD Press can be purchased by visiting ATD's
website at www.td.org/books or by calling 800.628.2783 or 703.683.8100.

Library of Congress Control Number: 2016951833

ISBN-10: 1-56286-640-0
ISBN-13: 978-1-56286-640-2
e-ISBN: 978-1-60728-113-9

**ATD Press Editorial Staff**
Director: Kristine Luecker
Manager: Christian Green
Community of Practice Manager, Learning & Development: Amanda Smith
Developmental Editor: Jack Harlow
Text Design: Iris Sanchez
Cover Design: Derek Thornton, Faceout Studio

Printed by Versa Press, Inc., East Peoria, IL

# CONTENTS

# PREFACE: WHERE IT ALL BEGAN

As practitioners who design workplace learning experiences, we share a passion for transforming workplace learning to appeal to learner curiosity, influence behavior change, and generate meaningful, relevant experiences. Throughout our careers as learning professionals, we have observed a tendency of resistance to learning among those who seemed skeptical about workplace training in general. Some of the assumptions we witnessed include training classes are a waste of time; the content is generic and doesn't help with individual roles and responsibilities; and learners don't feel engaged in training in a personally meaningful and productive way.

Learning through experience is one of the most natural, basic concepts of learning. It's how we begin to understand the world as children, and we continue learning through and reflecting upon experiences throughout our lives: "Learning is a process whereby the individual reacts to, learns from, and builds on experiences. [John Dewey] posited experiences are continuous in that they build on each other, each one affecting future experiences. Continuity signifies that each experience influences a person whether it is for better or for worse" (Monk 2013, 65). As adults, many of us carry around stereotypes and negative associations toward training. Some of these beliefs stem from the learning experiences we had as young students in school.

As a child, Jillian (co-founder 1) was often bored and disengaged at school. She was bright but struggled through much of her education, failing to see its applicability to the real world as her teachers lectured to her and her classmates. Years later, after graduating with a BS in management, Jillian was thrust into a role as a training director for Goodwill Industries, tasked with helping underemployed or unemployed people re-enter the workforce. Knowing nothing at the time about instructional design and given little direction, she thought back to the best teachers she'd had. "The less they talked, the more I learned," she recalled. Unwilling to perpetuate the ineffective lecturing methods that had affected what she learned and determined to make a difference in the lives of her students, she experimented with self-taught methods of active learning, taking note of which approaches worked best. And thus began her lifelong love affair with transforming the learning experience.

Shannon (co-founder 2) also found herself immersed in the world of learning from a young age. As an avid observer of human connections, she practiced being a teacher as a child and spent her days writing detailed stories of life laden with emotional experiences. With her BA in English, she began her career as a technical writer focusing on the end user, advocating that learners should get the information they need when they need it. As she moved into instructional design, she strove to ensure that each individual's learning needs were met clearly, simply, and effectively.

By the time we formed Idea Learning Group, it had become all too clear that learners in the workplace were generally no better off than students in the classroom who—not unlike Jillian as a child—were subject to ineffective and outdated learning methods. For us, these outdated learning methods seemed to have been carried over as the default training option for most learning professionals, including ourselves. We had to figure out a new way of approaching learning at work.

❃ ❃ ❃

It was the week before a big presentation for our local ATD chapter conference in 2012, and for the past month, we'd spent hours putting together a carefully crafted presentation covering the science of learning, one of our favorite topics. But as Shannon reviewed the materials for our presentation, it suddenly became strikingly clear: We were caught in a pickle. The slides were beautifully designed. The presentation was thorough. We knew the material inside and out.

There was just one big problem. It became increasingly clear to us that we were about to violate the very principles of brain-based learning that we'd set out to teach. Research has shown that people learn best through active, experiential, and social learning that is broken up into small and meaningful chunks. And yet here we were, clicking through slide after slide of information, lecturing to an imaginary audience on how to design brain-friendly learning programs.

We couldn't believe it. We weren't sure how we hadn't seen it before.

After all, we founded Idea Learning Group with the mission to improve the way people learn at work. We were progressive, forward thinking, and passionate about learning. So how was it that we now found ourselves here, violating the very rules we'd set out to champion?

We panicked. We had only a short amount of time until the conference, not enough to change the format of our presentation, our team advised. Besides, presenting any other way seemed risky, especially in front of a group of our peers. What if a new approach didn't work? What if we tried it, only to be laughed at by our fellow learning professionals? Regardless of how well founded a new approach might be, it's uncomfortable to step outside your comfort zone.

The clock was ticking.

Over the weekend, we both stressed about how—or even if—we should reformat our upcoming presentation on the science of learning, when an idea came to Jillian. Like many ideas, it wasn't entirely new. Years before, it had surfaced in a sudden moment of inspiration before quickly getting buried by the day-to-day responsibilities of life and work. Just like that, the idea had disappeared—until this particular Monday morning.

With the lightbulb in full blaze, we decided our plan of action. Before we'd even taken off our coats or poured our morning cup of tea, we gathered our team together.

"We're scratching everything," we announced. "We're starting over, and this is what we're going to do."

We detailed our vision: an interactive, play-based, experiential model that would allow learners to freely move around the room at their own speed and pace. Everything we'd discovered in our research—active learning, social learning, experiential learning, play—would be included.

And then for the important part: It would be station based, allowing learners to freely choose among the activities we'd prepared for them. Choice, we'd determined, was the component that most distinguished Cafeteria Learning from other models in the industry, even from more progressive approaches that were active and social.

We were invigorated, inspired, and ready to go.

As our team looked back at us, wide-eyed, it was apparent they thought we were crazy. But as we continued to explain our idea, they slowly began to see the potential, eventually giving way to unbridled enthusiasm.

We spent the next several days overhauling our presentation, transforming slides of lecture-based content into an array of hands-on, social activities and designing 15 different stations for learners to choose from (see chapter 10 for examples). We were nervous about trying a new approach, but we knew there was no turning back. We had the acute sense that maybe—just maybe—we were onto something. We had to find out.

When the big day arrived, we took a deep breath and introduced learners to our concept of Cafeteria Learning. Then, we let the participants loose to explore the learning stations. As they moved around to the various stations, we watched carefully to gauge their reactions. Were they enjoying themselves and engaging in the activities and with one another? Most important, were they learning?

We thought so, but even so, we were anxious. Our fears were finally quelled when a woman walked up to us after the workshop.

"I have to tell you," she started, as our hearts skipped a beat. "That was one of the best trainings I've ever attended." Then, she gave us a hug. Several other attendees came up to us after the event with positive feedback, too.

From that moment, we knew we were onto something. And that's how Cafeteria Learning was born, as an alternative or complement to traditional training. In practice, it's an approach to learning that allows instructional designers (chefs) to apply content (ingredients) to a variety of interchangeable activities (recipes), resulting in an informal classroom workshop in which each learner builds a customized learning experience (meal). It's our answer to passive, choiceless training that has become the norm.

You want to see learners light up, not shut down. You want learners to choose from a cornucopia of learning experiences rather than being force-fed learning. You want to see your company reap the benefits of well-executed training programs rather than grumble about their ineffectiveness. You want to transform workplace learning for the better. Read on to learn how.

## Acknowledgments

We would like to thank Lisa Rebagliati, MEd, for her contributions to this book. Many thanks as well to the ATD Cascadia Chapter, particularly Chapter President Grant Axtell and Executive Director Kathleen Bergquist. Finally, our thanks go out to the amazing team at Idea Learning Group: Adriane Jones, Arianna Nassib, Emily Segel, Katie Paulson, and Jennie Fennelle.

# INTRODUCTION

Imagine a world in which restaurants gave you only one choice. "This is what you're getting, and you'd better like it!" the waiter snarls as he places a plate of spaghetti in front of you. You used to love dining out—until now.

"Ugh. I hate spaghetti," you think to yourself as you pick up your fork to begin the less than exciting task of chewing your food. You feel more like a 5-year-old being force-fed your daily serving of vegetables than an adult enjoying a pleasant night out on the town.

We cannot help but cringe when we imagine a world of choice-less restaurants—not only because we like food way too much, but also because this scenario resembles today's learning and development field. Most organizations serve up learning programs that, even when masterfully prepared, lack an essential ingredient: choice.

Think about it. A chef may meticulously plan and carefully concoct a meal. She may prepare it with the very best ingredients, but not everyone will like it. One meal simply cannot meet everyone's needs.

Because most restaurants offer many options, ordering spaghetti—or chicken salad, or spicy fajitas—becomes an active choice rather than a reluctant "have to." Choice allows for a variety of tastes and dining preferences, ensuring as optimal an experience as possible. Spaghetti may very well still be on the menu—in fact, you may even end up choosing it—but you have a choice to select it, which makes all the difference.

This is precisely the active, engaging experience that the Cafeteria Learning model promotes. Cafeteria Learning brings together the best of the experiential, constructivist, and action learning approaches and bakes in an important brain-based twist: choice. What if instead of walking into a training event and seeing rows of chairs with an instructor waiting at the front of the room, your learners were surprised to find interactive stations stocked with hands-on materials? What if instead of sitting and listening to a lecturer read off words on presentation slides, your learners were free to explore and absorb the content at their own speed and direction? And what if instead of being given only one option for learning, your learners could choose from a variety of learner-centered activities, just like they might choose from a variety of food in a cafeteria?

*Let Them Choose* is written for you, the learning professional who is searching for another way to design learning experiences. Cafeteria Learning typically works best with what may be referred to as "soft skills" or "people skills" content such as communication, sales, time management, or goal setting. What makes this type of content work well with Cafeteria Learning is that it can be presented in a nonlinear way. That is, it doesn't matter what order the learner achieves the learning objectives, only that they are all met by the end of the learning experience. In contrast, "hard skills" training is intended to improve a learner's technical skill set in a very specific way. The Cafeteria Learning model could be applied to a training program for technical procedures, though how you structure and outline the activities around the learning objective might need more order.

Over the course of this book, we will present a start-to-finish guide on what Cafeteria Learning is and how to implement it within your organization.

In chapter 1, "How We Learn," we'll introduce research on how the brain learns best (perhaps unsurprisingly, it's the opposite of how many organizations structure their training). You'll learn why moving around a room and learning experientially is so much more powerful than sitting in your seat, how learners construct knowledge, and how choice enhances the learning process.

In chapter 2, "What Is Cafeteria Learning?" you'll gain an in-depth understanding of Cafeteria Learning and each of its components. You'll learn how Cafeteria Learning works, and the core components of a Cafeteria Learning workshop. And you'll see what it's like for a learner to move through a Cafeteria Learning experience.

Chapter 3, "Getting Buy-in for Cafeteria Learning," explores the process of getting organizational buy-in for your Cafeteria Learning program. You'll learn how Cafeteria Learning benefits the learner, the organization, and the learning professional.

Chapter 4, "Writing Cafeteria Learning Objectives," details a step-by-step tutorial on the art of writing Cafeteria Learning–specific learning objectives. You'll learn how to identify your three core learning objectives and write them in a manner that allows for sufficient choice.

Next, in chapter 5, "Designing Cafeteria Learning Activities," you'll discover the four-step process for designing Cafeteria Learning activities that revolve around each of your core learning objectives. You'll learn about the best way to brainstorm and select activities and why it's important to design activities that span various learning experiences to enhance the choice you offer your learners.

Chapter 6, "The Framework," covers the process for framing your content. You'll learn how to design a priming activity that engages learners from the start. You'll learn how to weave in foundational content that leads learners into the main activity workshop. And you'll learn how to bring your workshop to a close with a debriefing activity that helps your learners synthesize and reflect on what they've learned.

Chapter 7, "Facilitating Cafeteria Learning," shares tips and best practices for facilitating a successful Cafeteria Learning workshop. You'll learn how to prepare for facilitating a Cafeteria Learning workshop one month, one week, one day, and one hour before your workshop. You'll learn what you need to take into account when setting up your room and materials. And you'll learn the best way to introduce a Cafeteria Learning workshop and lead learners through the activities.

Chapter 8, "Measuring and Evaluating the Results," lays out helpful practices for evaluating your Cafeteria Learning workshop and gathering valuable feedback and metrics after your workshop has come to a close. You'll learn that evaluating the results of Cafeteria Learning is just as important as measuring more traditional learning experiences.

Chapter 9, "Case Studies," details how organizations have successfully used Cafeteria Learning to deliver engaging workshops. Through case studies, you'll learn about the intended learning outcomes, activity examples, and the perspectives from participants and stakeholders on their experiences learning with this method.

Finally, chapter 10, "Cafeteria Learning Activities," provides a hand-picked selection of our favorite Cafeteria Learning activities, which you can use as a starting point for your own design process.

We hope *Let Them Choose* will inspire you to take meaningful steps toward creating learning experiences in your organization that effectively harness the power of choice and ensure that each individual's learning needs are met. Cafeteria Learning is the model we've designed for achieving this goal. We hope you'll join us on our quest to transform workplace learning through the power of choice.

# 1

# HOW WE LEARN

"If keeping someone's attention in a lecture were a business it would have an 80% failure rate," wrote John Medina, author of *Brain Rules: 12 Principles for Surviving and Thriving at Work, Home, and School,* in 2008.

Stop and think about that statistic for a moment. In any other area of business, an 80 percent failure rate would be unacceptable. Imagine that 80 percent of your company's products had defects, 80 percent of your deliveries failed to reach the consumer on time, or 80 percent of the time you were late to work. That wouldn't be acceptable, right?

Yet that's precisely what's happening in workplaces worldwide.

The more we observed the ineffectiveness of traditional lecture-based training, the more we began to wonder: If the status quo isn't working, what does it really take to optimize the learning experience? If learners don't learn best in a lecture, how do they learn best?

What about learning preferences? When asked, most learners express a preference for how they like information to be presented to them—auditory, visual, or kinesthetic, for example. Many factors influence an individual's learning preference, such as past educational experiences, social environment, or basic cognitive structure. Could learning preferences be as varied as individuals themselves?

These questions both fascinated us and drove us to find the answer.

We hit the streets—on the way to the library—to find better ways to facilitate adult learning in the workplace. We reviewed several existing educational theories, devouring the research on brain science and psychology as it relates to learning. We aren't brain-based learning experts, but we have amassed a vast reservoir of knowledge about optimal learning practices. Below we've provided several sample approaches to adult learning, each of which influenced our eventual development of Cafeteria Learning: a model for active, social, and experiential learning that focuses on choice.

## Experiential Learning

*A little girl stands in the middle of a driveway, her face beaming with excitement. Today is the day her father has promised to teach her to ride her bike.*

*After a few minutes her dad makes his way outside and exclaims with a smile, "Time for bike riding lessons!" He then proceeds to take his daughter's hand and leads her inside the house, where a slide presentation is cued up.*

*"OK. Have a seat, please," Dad instructs. He shines his laser pointer onto the projector screen. "Today we're going to talk about the four steps of riding a bike. Pay careful attention—your mother and I will be testing you on this later!"*

*He gives her a handout and begins to read aloud from the slide presentation:*

*"With the right amount of effort and practice, riding a bike can be easy and fun! Here are the four steps you must know in order to get started."*

*"Step one: Always wear a helmet."*

*"Step two: Stand to the left or right of the bike with the handlebars firmly gripped."*

*"Step three: Lift your leg over the bar and sit on the seat. Your tippy-toes should just barely reach the ground . . ."*

OK, so perhaps this story is a little far-fetched, but it beautifully illustrates a simple point: Learning without experience isn't natural. We wouldn't learn to ride a bike this way, so why would we expect our employees to learn this way?

Not only does it make sense that we learn best through experience, but it is also scientifically accurate: The very physiology of our brains is wired to learn through experience. Learning through experience is one of the most natural, basic concepts of learning. It's how we begin to understand the world as children, and it's how we continue learning through, and reflecting upon, experiences throughout our lives.

"While genetics and prenatal influences may calibrate the brain at birth, it is largely dependent on subsequent experiences to determine its capacities and deficiencies," explained Kenneth Wesson in a 2010 article for *Brain World* magazine. "Author Joseph Epstein stated, 'We are what we read.' Neuroscientists would assert, 'We are what we experience.' Neural circuits are constantly reorganized and rerouted, based on the quantity, quality and timing of our experiences."

Until recently, the common assumption was that our brains, like the rest of our bodies, stopped developing when we became adults. It was believed that neural cell generation—or neurogenesis—was not possible after childhood. We now know that neurogenesis is possible, albeit to a lesser extent, throughout adulthood (Ernst and Frisén 2015). "Although we cannot regenerate limbs, we can re-invent our brains through neuro-plasticity. . . . Changes in brain function occur as the brain re-wires itself in response to new demands placed on it by the external environment. Our malleable brains help us thrive by crafting environmentally appropriate survival strategies. Brain plasticity underlies the brain's extraordinary capacity to learn, unlearn and relearn," Wesson wrote.

Enter David Kolb, an American educational theorist who developed a learning theory known as experiential learning. "Learning is the process whereby knowledge is created through the transformation of experience. Knowledge results from the combination of grasping experience and transforming it" (Kolb 1984, 41). Experiential learning "emphasizes the central role that experience plays in the learning process and regards learning as a holistic process of adaptation to the world, which involves the integrated functioning of the total organism—thinking, feeling, perceiving and behaving" (Li, Mobley, and Kelley 2013, 34-35). It consists of a "direct encounter with the phenomena being studied rather than merely thinking about the encounter, or only considering the possibility of doing something about it" (Borzak 1981).

Many well-known figures support the idea of learning through experience and have accordingly developed their own models for providing stimulating experiential learning environments. Maria Montessori, for example, an Italian physician and educator known for developing discovery-based schools across the world, built a movement that started in the early 1900s but truly blossomed in the 1960s. The Montessori model emphasized "opportunities for student movement and interaction in a structured environment that supports children's natural curiosity" (Ultanir 2012, 204). In Montessori schools, children learn through direct experience and work with physical materials rather than receiving formal instruction (through lectures).

Consider this excerpt from Glenn Rifkin's 2013 article (59) on the benefits of a Montessori education: "Daniel H. Pink believes that using Montessori methods in corporate training is an idea whose time has come. Using Montessori methods in corporate training 'would require people to unlearn some bad habits they've acquired in other types of formal education,' Pink said. 'If Montessori-style internal training isn't already happening,' he declared, 'someone should start it.'"

"Scientific observation," wrote Montessori, "has established that education is not what the teacher gives; education is a natural process spontaneously carried out by the human individual, and is acquired not by listening to words but by experiences upon the environment" (Montessori 1946, 3).

Brain expert Eric Jensen wrote in his book, *Brain-Based Learning: The New Science of Teaching & Training*, "The brain is not very good at absorbing countless bits of semantic (factual) information. What feeds the brain more is meaningful exposure to larger models, patterns, and experiences. . . . This is why it makes good brain sense to facilitate a variety of experiences from which students can extract their own learning. The proportion of time that learners ought to be doing and talking, rather than sitting and listening, is a proportion of several variables" (Jensen 2000, 34-35).

Experience—doing, acting, touching, feeling, moving—is a natural and essential part of effective learning. It enhances our ability to learn, remember, and understand.

## Emotional Learning

Think about one of your earliest memories. Can you see it in your mind? What does it feel like, sound like; who is there? Why do you remember this particular experience and not almost everything else that has happened since then? Did this event have a strong emotional component?

Let's say you're in charge of creating a program that influences a change in behavior—for example, reducing texting and driving. You can create a slide presentation that provides a list of bullet points as to why driving and texting is bad, or you can display an image of a wrecked car with a reminder to avoid texting and driving. Which do you think will evoke more emotion? Which do you think will come to the driver's mind as he decides whether to text and drive? Why?

Emotion acts as the framework that learners use to interpret meaning: According to Priscilla Vail (1994), the late prominent expert on learning, "Emotion is the on-off switch for learning." We make thousands of decisions every day based on our emotions. Events that cause a significant emotional response tend to stick in our minds long after the experience has ended. As with your earliest childhood memories, you're more likely to invoke an emotional response with learners—and consequently a memory—by displaying an image of a wrecked car than if you displayed just the words. Emotions influence how we learn. Perhaps the topic you design training for doesn't have the same obvious emotional potential as the texting and driving example, but if you can insert humor, sarcasm, anxiety, joy, or some other emotion into your content, you can use it to your advantage and create a memorable learning experience.

Eric Jensen (2000) also noted that emotions:
- Help us figure out what's real and what we believe and feel.
- Activate long-term memory (the more intense the amygdala arousal, the stronger the imprint).
- Help us engage our values while making decisions.

Unlike rational decision making, which eliminates feelings and relies on pros and cons, modern brain research casts a new light on the important role of emotions in learning and decision making. According to research by the Center for Development and Learning, the brain relies on basic emotions—fear, anger, sadness—to urge action (Lawson 2002). Emotions start in a complex bundle of nerves in the middle part of our brain called the limbic system. It's here where our emotions are housed and memories are formed. When this system is operating, the pathway to learning is open.

One of the structures in the limbic system is located deeper in the brain. The amygdala, two almond-shaped groups of nuclei, performs a primary role in the processing of memory, decision making, and emotional reactions. In response to internal and external stimuli, the amygdala releases chemicals that stimulate our brain, which can help us process and remember information.

Effective learning, then, should be designed to arouse emotional responses within learners—to open the pathways in their brains to learning. Doing this should help learners remember important information and take action on the concepts they've learned.

## Social Learning

A tidal wave of social learning is reshaping the way we experience new information. Social learning builds a sense of community, creates standards or reference points, and offers alternative perspectives. It also generates support and encouragement within our networks. Children, of course, seem to learn through social interaction quite naturally. Perhaps social learning allows us to tap into something fundamental to learning: a sense of curiosity and exploration.

Many of us spend a lot of time on social media through sites such as Facebook, Twitter, and Pinterest. Then when we go to work, it's as if we revert back to how we used to communicate a decade ago. With email as the standard mode of communication at work, it's often difficult to openly communicate and collaborate on projects. "Training gives people solutions to problems already solved. Collaboration addresses challenges no one has overcome before," wrote Tony Bingham and Marcia Conner, co-authors of *The New Social Learning: Connect. Collaborate. Work.* (2015). "When you engage with people, you build your own insight into what's being discussed. Someone else's understanding complements yours, and together you start to weave an informed interpretation. You tinker until you can move on."

As journalist Debra Donston-Miller (2012) says, you should "embrace social learning or be left behind." Learners have grown tired of searching for information online; now they want to network with and learn from their peers. Effective learning is not a one-sided transaction in which knowledge is transferred from an instructor, presentation, or textbook directly to the learner. The information learners can glean from networking and interacting with one another is often as valuable, if not more so, than the information they will receive from traditional learning methods.

## Learning for Introverts and Extroverts

In our experience, the terms *introverts* and *extroverts* have become hot topics in learning and development. If you've ever taken the Myers-Briggs Type Indicator, you probably know which personality type you most strongly identify with. It's all about how you naturally derive your energy and process information. Extroverts generate their energy from an active group, while introverts thrive in solitude and reflection.

As with any sort of sociological labeling, there's a high risk for misunderstanding and stereotyping. For example, introverts aren't necessarily shy. In *Quiet*, Susan Cain (2012) provides an in-depth analysis of the introverted life. "Shyness is the fear of negative judgment, while introversion is simply the preference for less stimulation. Shyness is inherently uncomfortable; introversion is not," Cain says. And extroverts don't always talk before or in place of thinking.

At a meeting of local learning and development professionals, we facilitated a lively discussion about our experiences designing training programs with introverts in mind. The majority of individuals at the meeting self-identified as introverts, which is the opposite of American culture at large. We discussed some of the common misunderstandings and stereotypes for both introverts and extroverts. Table 1-1 illustrates what the group said.

Table 1-1. Misunderstandings of Extroverts and Introverts

| Extroverts | Introverts |
|---|---|
| Talk just to hear themselves talk | Are underdeveloped extroverts |
| Take over the room | Are lonely and/or selfish |
| Think they have the best ideas | Are not good leaders |
| Are always trying to change introverts into extroverts | Are lazy or withdrawn |

When we shifted the discussion from misunderstandings and stereotypes to a self-reported discussion of how introverts prefer to experience learning, we saw some really interesting results.

Our group of introverts told us that they prefer learning that:
- takes place in small groups
- offers pre-exposure to content before group discussion
- is discovery-based, and as much as possible is self-paced
- offers built-in opportunities for reflection and follow-up discussions
- is free from distractions and overstimulation
- allows for a balance of quiet time and some interaction
- provides an opportunity for sharing information in pairs
- includes time for independent reflection.

Much of what we found is supported by research cited in Susan Cain's book.

In addition, consider what psychologist Russell G. Geen found in a 1980s study of introverts and extroverts: Participants were asked to play a challenging word game while being periodically interrupted with a burst of noise. They were given headsets with the ability to adjust the volume until it was "just right" for them. Extroverts chose more intense noise levels, while introverts reduced the level of noise. And then extroverts and introverts performed best when they adjusted the volume of the noise to a volume they preferred (Geen 1984). When they were asked to switch headsets, but keep the preferred volume of the other personality type, performance results of both extroverts and introverts went down.

The question is how can we design learning experiences in which introverts don't have to feel dominated by extroverts and where they are free to learn in their preferred style and manner (and vice versa)? An effective and comprehensive learning experience appeals to both introverts and extroverts, not just to one or the other. Offering learners a choice in the activities they prefer to participate in is one way to achieve this.

## Learning Through Play as Adults

Learning through play is a given for children, so why do we have a hard time accepting play as an effective means of learning as adults? Why do we so often dismiss it as a waste of time? According to authors Patrick Bateson and Paul Martin in *Play, Playfulness, Creativity and Innovation* (2013), many species continue to play beyond their youth. Play is one way to spread discoveries through social learning. In fact, some animals such as rats and grizzly bears fail to properly develop socially without a healthy amount of play.

In an October 2014 article in *Chief Learning Officer*, Andrea Park looked at problem solving through the lens of play, particularly gamification. She cited research by the Wharton School at the University of Pennsylvania indicating that there are eight steps to promote business success in workplace gamification: "Problem solving, exploration, teamwork, recognition, success, surprise and novelty, creativity and knowledge sharing." She continued, "Interactive learning programs at millennial-friendly companies often provide examples of several, if not all, of these qualities."

Play is one of nature's ways for generating new neural networks and reconciling cognitive difficulties, according to a 2009 article in *U.S. News & World Report*. It's not only a useful way to solve problems, but it also helps us build our creativity and social relationships, according to Stuart Brown and Christopher Vaughan in their book *Play: How It Shapes the Brain, Opens the Imagination, and Invigorates the Soul* (2010).

Learning, it seems, doesn't always have to be hard work. We believe you can add levity and fun without compromising instructional goals.

## Lecturing on Its Own Is Ineffective

Imagine you are in a dimly lit conference room, coffee in hand, feet on the ground, sitting face-forward. You watch as an instructor walks up to the podium, clears her throat, and begins to speak.

Ten minutes in, she's lost you. As she lectures on, you find yourself thinking about lunch—should you stay at the office and finish the project you're working on, or go out with co-workers for lunch? Did you remember to lock the front door this morning? Hope the dog doesn't get into the trash.

The people on either side of you aren't faring much better. You watch as they check their smartphones, fidget in their seats, and do their best to appear semi-interested. You feel like a life-sized replica of those bobble-heads on a car dashboard, continuously nodding off despite your best efforts to stay alert.

This style of instruction does not offer the opportunity for interaction or the opportunity to actively apply the concepts in meaningful ways. There's no opportunity for input, reflection, or new ideas, and certainly no opportunity to choose among learning options. Your only option, in fact, is to sit in your chair, attempt to keep your eyes open, and resist the urge to jot down your grocery list.

The purpose of the training, you'd been told, was to generate excitement about new company initiatives and boost morale. And yet it failed on all accounts. The worst part is this type of training doesn't just happen in bad dreams. Training like this takes place every day, where lecturers drone on, time ticks slowly, and learners check out.

It isn't surprising that lecturing is often ineffective. After all, the word *lecture* is rooted in the Latin word *legere*, "to read." In medieval universities, before the invention of mechanical printing, the professor would stand at the lectern and read aloud from handmade texts (Wood 1989). The lecture was born because books were rare, valuable, and in short supply—in other words, it was born out of necessity, not because it was an effective way to teach.

That said, lecturing can be done well. Lectures and slide presentations aren't inherently bad; in some cases they are quite useful. In fact, we often begin our Cafeteria Learning sessions with mini-lectures to provide learners with context and a foundation for the rest of the workshop. The key is to treat lectures as one piece of the overall learning experience rather than relying on them as the sole method of content delivery—and to do so skillfully based on brain-based principles that have been shown to keep learners engaged.

TED Talks are a wonderful example of engaging lectures. They owe their success in part to their brief format; the rule is no longer than 18 minutes, told by people with a palpable passion for their topic.

## Constructivist Learning

"We do not learn by passively receiving, and then remembering what we are taught," wrote Geoff Petty, author of *Evidence-Based Teaching*. "Instead, learning involves actively constructing our own meanings. This literally involves the construction of connections between neurons. We invent our own concepts and ideas, linked to what we already know. This 'meaning-making' theory of learning is called 'constructivism'" (Petty n.d., 1).

Petty explained that "exam howlers," or entertaining mistakes made on exams by children, are an effective illustration of constructivism in action. One student, for example, stated that "history calls them 'Romans' because they never stayed in one place for very long" (Petty n.d., 1).

"These genuine mistakes show 'meaning making' in practice," wrote Petty. "If students only remembered what they were told, they would not make such mistakes; they would either remember or not. Conceptual errors show that we make our own mental constructs, we don't just remember other peoples'" (Petty n.d., 1).

Our brains actively interpret and construct, rather than passively receive, knowledge based on what we already know. Of course, even when learning from a lecture we are constructing knowledge on some level. But by giving learners the opportunity to construct their own knowledge rather than spoon-feeding them preconstructed information, we take learning to the next level. And the more opportunities learners are given to actively construct their own knowledge, the stronger their learning becomes.

This concept will make intuitive sense to anyone who's ever purchased ready-to-assemble furniture. Consider the following question: If someone gave you a piece of furniture to assemble and then explained to you how they put it together, how well would you remember what they'd told you five minutes later? A day later? A few weeks later? What's more, how well would you understand why it was built in a particular way and the underlying concepts of its construction?

In this way, knowledge is like building furniture: If we really want people to build meaningful and relevant learning experiences, we must allow them to construct it themselves and to draw their own conclusions from the pieces they're given. "It is not the knowledge or ideas, but the learner's construction of knowledge or ideas that is critical. Increases in student learning follow a reconceptualization as well as an acquisition of information," said John Hattie (2009, 37).

This idea is at the heart of the constructivist approach, which is rooted in research and theories developed by innovative educators and psychologists such as John Dewey and Jean Piaget. "Only by wrestling with the conditions of the problem at hand, seeking and finding his own solution (not in isolation but in correspondence with the teacher and other pupils) does one learn," said Dewey in his 1910 book, *How We Think*.

The constructivist approach emphasizes learning over teaching, offers authentic tasks to engage learners, provides opportunities to construct instead of reproduce information, and poses problem-based scenarios (Ultanir 2012).

# The Missing Piece: Choice

In a nutshell, effective learning takes places when experience becomes central—when learners have the chance to act, move, problem solve, and construct their own knowledge. So how do we apply this to our work?

"Corporate learning should be characterized by sharing knowledge, capturing experiences, reusing them, creating new knowledge, and recognizing and solving workplace problems in a process-oriented, collaborative manner," stated researchers Betty Collis and Anoush Margaryan (2004, 39). We've been proponents of this kind of learning for years. However, as much success as we had with these approaches, we'd occasionally notice something interesting: Certain activities worked better for some learners and not for others—some thrived in group activities, while others preferred to learn alone. If learners felt uncomfortable about speaking aloud in a group setting or competing against others, it actually ended up hindering their learning. Or the thought of what would be required of them prevented others from showing up to the workshop all together.

Still others seemed to lack motivation and enthusiasm for the assigned activity. Despite the hands-on approach, some learners felt as if someone were forcing them to participate (though technically, someone was). Despite their increased engagement when compared with a traditional lecture, it still seemed like some subtle but nonetheless important piece was missing from many current approaches.

As we continued our quest to understand how people learn, we figured out what was missing: choice. Learners thrive when the learning approach not only adheres to the principles summarized thus far, but also when it allows them to choose from a variety of ways to experience the content. In fact, increasing learners' options and choices in turn increases their intrinsic motivation (Zuckerman et al. 1978).

Most learning experiences, whether active, including activities, or passive, as in lecturing, are akin to eating out at a choice-less restaurant. Rather than feeling empowered and in control, learners often feel as if they're being forced to learn in one way. And when they feel as if they're no longer in the driver's seat, they understandably demonstrate apathy, resistance, and dread.

Choice is important for other reasons. Research has shown that grouping learners by one learning style and catering a learning program to it is ineffective—everyone learns through various modalities (Looss 2001). The preference for one learning style over another can shift over the course of a person's lifetime or even within a single day. What research on learning styles does emphasize, however, is that providing a choice of learning experiences is compatible with how we learn best: "Rather than trying to figure out who is what kind of learner, the [learner style] framework is most valuable in its ability to help you determine if your teaching approaches and methodologies cover the broad spectrum of learner types. . . . The two most important things to remember for building a successful brain-based learning styles approach are: (1) provide a variety of approaches, and (2) offer choices," states Jensen (2000, 146). Jensen suggests providing choice among multiple learning characteristics within the following categories:

- context variables (for example, contextual "real life" environments or structured classroom environments; individual or group learning)
- input preferences (for example, visual, auditory, or kinesthetic input sources)
- processing formats (for example, "big picture" learning or sequenced, formulaic learning; abstract learning or concrete learning)
- response filters (for example, learning through noting similarities or noting differences; learning by trial and error or reflection).

As we sought to design the ultimate Cafeteria Learning experience, we embraced Jensen's research on how to blend choice into any learning offering. In addition, our model took inspiration from the Universal Design for Learning principles, which aim to give all participants equal access to learning opportunities, as defined by the Center for Applied Special Technology (CAST 2000). One such principle reinforces the need for choice in any learning setting: "Offering learners choices can develop self-determination, pride in accomplishment, and increase the degree to which they feel connected to their learning." But the principles caution that this choice should not extend to the learning objective itself; learners need some structure in what they need to achieve as a result of the learning program. Finally, much like learners prefer choices in how they learn, they also have preferences for how much and what kind of choices they want.

When you design your own Cafeteria Learning style training program, you cannot solely focus on providing choice. You must also prioritize the right kinds of choices and determine how much autonomy learners should have to ensure engagement with the learning material and change when they return to their daily work. In the end, the optimal learning environment empowers learners to own their learning experience— Cafeteria Learning and the framework within this book can be your guide to this lofty goal.

## Summary

For a long time, we struggled to integrate everything we'd learned into one approach. How could we provide learning that was experiential, social, playful, active, and constructive? How could we cater to both extroverts and introverts? Like many learning professionals, we felt stretched for time. Sometimes it felt easier to default to the norm and continue doing things the way they'd always been done.

That, of course, is what had gotten us into this dilemma in the first place. Like most learning professionals, we can relate to having a lot of work to do and not enough time, or working in environments where the way it's always been done is the expectation. So we defaulted to the familiar, traditional instructional approaches, even when we set out with the best intentions to transform the way people learn at work.

But now we had a choice: Walk the walk and risk an unknown (and potentially disastrous) outcome in front of our peers, or violate the very principles and values we stood for.

Something had to give.

# 2

# WHAT IS CAFETERIA LEARNING?

Think of Cafeteria Learning as a complete dining experience rather than a grab-n-go meal. With Cafeteria Learning you begin with an appetizer (priming), move on to the main course (activities), and finish with dessert (debrief).

Cafeteria Learning workshops begin with a priming activity that engages learners and gets them thinking about the content. This not only prepares learners for the learning that's to come, but it's also a great way to involve learners from the get-go and make use of the often overlooked first few minutes of a workshop when learners are settling in.

Research shows that priming, or providing advance knowledge of the information to come, increases learners' abilities to retrieve this information in the future (Martin and Turennout 2002) and also activates an important problem-solving area of the brain (Carter, MacDonald, and Ursu 2000). "Priming works to retrieve information from memory when a priming stimulus is presented and sets off a chain of events in which one node of a concept is linked to another," wrote Dosher and Rosedale (1989). Ratcliff and McKoon (1988, 405) suggested that "if the prime is directly related to the target concept, the individual will have an easier time recalling the concept as a chunk of information."

The workshop officially begins with the main course, during which learners spend the most time freely choosing, exploring, and engaging in learning activities at their own pace. Stations are set up around the room where learners get to decide which learning activities they want to participate in. Each activity is designed to provide the same content for learners to discover no matter which activity they choose. For the most part, the content, or knowledge, is in these learning activities. By taking a constructivist approach to learning, Cafeteria Learning allows learners to discover and construct their own knowledge as they complete the activities and interact with their colleagues and peers.

Lastly, each workshop ends with a dessert, or debriefing activity, that helps learners synthesize the content and reflect on what it means to them within the context of their day-to-day jobs. An effective debriefing, which facilitates collaborative reflection, can bridge the gap between the workshop content and applying learning back at work (Wick et al. 2006, 73).

The experience as a whole is exploratory, allowing learners to build, construct, and discover information and meaning for themselves rather than simply memorizing and reciting it. It emphasizes choice in activities that ultimately leads learners to the same learning outcome regardless of the activities they chose.

With Cafeteria Learning, we've carefully selected elements from each of the experiential, constructivist, and action learning theories, added in choice as a twist, and organized it all into an approach that encapsulates what we believe is the best of brain science and learning theory.

## A Cafeteria Learning Story

"Not another training," you grumble to yourself as you prepare to facilitate your company's workshop Creating an Inclusive Workplace.

As a seasoned corporate trainer, who's been with the company for years, you know exactly what to expect: You'll spend an afternoon inside a too-warm, too-packed meeting room as you explain the importance of an inclusive workplace. Maybe you'll sprinkle in a few discussion questions for good measure, which participants will reluctantly volunteer to answer: Their boss is in the room, after all. They better look engaged.

All you can think about is the fact that you have more important things to do: Between managing day-to-day operations and preparing for a critical quarter-end deadline, you're already squeezed for time. On top of everything else on your plate, your team is expanding and you're in the process of hiring a new consultant. You already know that having an inclusive workplace is one of the company values, and you will do your best to model it.

You review the facilitator guide. It's different. There will be interactive stations stocked with hands-on materials, and you're responsible for summarizing the priming activity and presenting foundational content for about 10 minutes of the allotted session time. You do a double take: Are those building bricks referenced as learning materials?

This couldn't be right.

You walk through the experience in your mind.

"Are you here for the Creating an Inclusive Workplace workshop?" you ask as participants arrive. You smile and direct them toward a table full of photos depicting a variety of people's faces.

You ask learners to pick a photo that appeals to them—any photo—and to use the first few minutes before the workshop begins to answer discussion questions that have been placed on their table with a partner.

Participants appear a tad nervous at first. It's much more comfortable to sit near the back of the room, listening to the lecture and occasionally taking some notes. But bit by bit, their curiosity helps them to overcome their nerves.

You imagine one of the learners sitting next to a manager from their department, saying good morning and agreeing to work together. One of the learners reads one of the provided discussion questions aloud: "Why do you think you picked the photo that you did?"

The learners had thought about why they picked it, but after reflecting for a moment, they realize that they'd selected a person who's just like them: Male. Caucasian. Similar in age. Do they do the same thing when choosing whom to engage with on their team? Although they'd never exclude anyone purposefully, it dawns on them for the first time that maybe they have an unconscious bias toward socializing and working with people who are similar. It's subtle and they mean no harm; it's just what comes naturally.

The learner thinks about Jenny, who's one of just a handful of women in the department, and wonders: Could this tendency to work more closely with the men on the team make Jenny feel excluded and undervalued?

"Ding!"

You ring a bell, signifying that the workshop is about to begin. The first five minutes of this experience has already sparked personal insights, and the workshop hasn't even officially started.

You begin, "Today we're using a learning technique called Cafeteria Learning. It's designed to give you the freedom to choose how you learn. Similar to a cafeteria, stations are set up around the room to offer you choices. You get to decide which learning activities you want to participate in. When it's time, you'll browse the activity menu (Figure 2-1), which lists your activity choices. First, let's talk a little bit about why we are here today, the expected learning outcome for the workshop, and what you will learn this morning."

"As you know fostering an inclusive workplace is one of our company values. I'd like to begin with a brief review of our organization's mission, vision, and values, and our philosophy around the importance of creating an inclusive workplace. Then I have just a couple of slides to show you."

After emphasizing the desired workshop outcomes and learning objectives, you continue, "Let's review your activity menu for today. It lists the learning activities you can select from during today's workshop."

You continue, "At the top of the menu are the three topics we are learning today, and under each topic there are three activities. You will choose one activity from each topic. The activities you choose are completely up to you. If you've completed one activity from each topic and you have extra time, feel free to choose additional activities.

"Don't worry about not learning something because you didn't complete all of the activities! Each activity has been designed to help you learn the same content within that topic, no matter which activities you choose.

Figure 2-1. Sample Activity Menu

| Choose at Least One Activity From Each Topic Below. If Time Allows, You May Complete More. | | |
| --- | --- | --- |
| Understanding Me | Understanding You | Understanding Strategies |
| Identify your communication preferences. | Seek to understand others. | Consider differing perspectives. |
| ☐ **Uniquely Me** <br> Draw an image of yourself that reflects your communication style. | ☐ **Telling My Story** <br> Record yourself telling a story about your experience understanding others. | ☐ **Case by Case** <br> Read and discuss scenarios and then reveal the correct answers. |
| ☐ **Who Am I?** <br> Share facts about yourself for each communication style. | ☐ **Stronger Together** <br> Construct a puzzle as you consider strengths of people you work with. | ☐ **Brick by Brick** <br> Plan and then construct a stable bridge. |
| ☐ **Dimensions of Me** <br> Write facts about yourself that reflect your communication style. | ☐ **Can't Judge a Book by Its Cover** <br> Flip a book to learn about the unique qualities of others. | ☐ **Communicate With Care** <br> Write your reaction and response to a conversation. |

"With that, take a moment to consider which activities interest you and make your selections. Then, you'll have a chance to participate at your own pace, and I'll let you know when you have 15 minutes left. Of course, I'll be checking in at each of the stations and available to answer any questions you may have."

You overhear a learner say to another, "This is going to be different." Although they aren't quite sure what to expect, they seem intrigued and also comforted by the fact that they're in control of their own learning.

Each activity menu is organized into three main topics, each of which has three related activities to choose from. Each topic and the three activities that relate to it is called a "learning topic."

You watch as participants head straight for their activities of choice. You notice one begins the "Brick by Brick" activity within the "Understanding Strategies" topic.

As you read deeper into the facilitator guide, you imagine the following scene:

The learner partners with Miguel from the finance department, whom she's never met before. "Whoever thought we'd get to play with building bricks at work?" she says to Miguel. "This is going to be fun!"

As they work together to build a unique structure, some differences in opinion arise; nevertheless, you can't help but notice how well Miguel's analytical mind complements Emily's: Her idea for the bridge is lofty and grand; his is sturdy, calculated, and realistic. Without her vision, the bridge would have lacked beauty and many value-added features. Without his analytical approach, however, the bridge would have been shoddy—it would have fallen to shambles. Realistically, she needed some healthy nuts-and-bolts perspective to make it work.

While answering the discussion questions, it dawns on them just how critical it is to communicate and share these unique perspectives, resources, and skills in the workplace, both inside the department and out. They discuss how they might work with other departments more closely so everyone can bring a unique perspective to the table and help solve problems affecting both departments—in the past they've always tried to solve problems individually or with their own teams.

You begin to think about the candidates you've been interviewing to fill your department's open position: Sure, you relate more easily to people who think like you, but could it be beneficial to bring someone on board with a completely different set of perspectives and skills?

Next, you move on to understanding the "Telling My Story" activity within the "Understanding You" topic. Using a tablet, learners record themselves relating a story about a time in which they witnessed or experienced inclusion not being valued. They also have the opportunity to view stories recorded by colleagues.

Learners sit down at the table, read the story prompt card, and record their story. When they're finished, they can review the other recordings. One such recording recounts an employee's personal story of moving to the United States from India:

> "I was in one of my first meetings with my prior company, and not everyone could understand my accent. I thought I had important contributions to make, but no one asked for clarification or further explanation—most of the time my comments were just skipped over or dismissed. It was easy to feel like my voice wasn't valued or heard. Eventually I just decided to stop contributing."

You think about this story and it triggers important questions and insights for you: Inside and outside of formal meetings, how are you making sure everyone on your team is given the chance to speak up and that they all feel heard? You realize that, purposefully or not, you tend to interact more with people who are similar to you. Why not purposefully create an environment of inclusion?

As learners are engrossed in the activities, participating in meaningful discussions, and reflecting on how they will behave differently and apply what they have learned to encourage inclusion on their team, you begin to understand the difference this method of learning provides. As a trainer you're no longer the "sage on the stage" but rather a facilitator to ensure that the framework is set for personal, meaningful learning.

As you near the end of the workshop, you bring the learners back together as a group to debrief each activity. You ask learners to volunteer to share some of their experiences and tie their insights back to the intended lesson for each topic. Listening to other's insights provides learners with even more to think about and apply.

New relationships with people within the company are formed, and initial nervousness has faded away. What was once abstract has suddenly become relevant, real, and meaningful. Learning that once felt mandatory and one-sided now feels like a choice. You provided the framework and foundational content while the learners constructed their own meaning and ideas that they'll apply, ones that are relevant to their particular experience and workplace.

At the close of the workshop, you invite learners to reflect on a final question, "Knowing what you know now, what will you do differently in your job?" They write their answer down on a pair of sticky notes: one to stick onto a collaborative board along with those of the rest of the group and one to take with them.

You think about what your answer would be, "Actively seek to embrace rather than ignore differences," which further crystallizes your understanding of how you can apply these concepts to your work. You thought you got it before, but now you really get it.

As you close the facilitator guide, you wonder, "Why didn't we do a workshop with activity choices like this 10 years ago?"

## Summary

Cafeteria Learning takes the best of what we learned in our research and experience and rolls it all together into one simple framework with choice at its core. Cafeteria Learning consists of three main components: an appetizer (priming activity), a main course (choose, explore, engage activities), and a dessert (debrief). Stations are set up around the room, and learners get to decide which learning activities they want to participate in. Each activity is designed to provide the same content for learners to discover no matter which activity they choose. By taking a constructivist approach to learning, Cafeteria Learning allows learners to discover and build their own knowledge as they complete the activities and interact with their colleagues and peers.

# 3

# GETTING BUY-IN FOR CAFETERIA LEARNING

So you're thinking about implementing Cafeteria Learning within your organization, but first you need to get approval from your company's stakeholders and executives. What are some of the best ways to do that? How have others done it? Could it really work for your organization?

Answering these questions starts with obtaining a deep understanding of the unique benefits Cafeteria Learning provides to the learner, the organization, and the learning professional. Let's explore each one of these in turn. Then we'll discuss common obstacles that often stand in the way of adopting a Cafeteria Learning approach, along with advice for overcoming them and getting buy-in from executives and organizational stakeholders.

## Benefits to the Learner

Chapter 1 discussed how learners' brains construct and retain knowledge best. The resulting benefits of applying this research are clear: Learners become deeply engaged in the learning process, finding it fun and enjoyable rather than tedious or unpleasant. Of course, they actually learn in ways that meaningfully influence their work:

> "I went into this morning's workshop wondering how I would sit still for two hours straight . . . and to my delight, the time flew by. The material was spot-on relevant, in my opinion. I loved how the scenarios were tailor-made for our company. The exercises were

fun and engaging, and it was nice to work with colleagues from outside my department. I feel like I got takeaways on some sensitive subjects."—*Cafeteria Learning workshop participant*

They also build relationships with their colleagues that may not have occurred otherwise.

"One [of the benefits] is the interaction with colleagues. Even if it's just 'I now know your name and where you work,' we have people who know each other now who didn't know each other before, whereas if we'd had a traditional training class and just sat down, they wouldn't necessarily know that person any better. There's a relationship and a camaraderie effect to this approach that is really a side benefit that you get by using it."—*Training and development manager*

But what other implications does this hold for learners? Let's dig a little deeper. What do learners really want from their jobs?

Daniel H. Pink, author of the *New York Times* bestselling book *Drive: The Surprising Truth About What Motivates Us,* argues that salary, benefits, and other similar perks (that is, extrinsic motivators) can only go so far in motivating employees. What they really want is the rich satisfaction of working in an environment that supports their deeper needs for autonomy, mastery, and purpose, allowing the joy of intrinsic motivation to surface.

- **Autonomy** means that workers have control and choice over how they reach a goal or complete a task. "Control leads to compliance; autonomy leads to engagement," writes Pink (2009, 110).
- Pink defines **mastery** as "the desire to get better and better at something that matters" (111). The drive toward mastery is innate within each one of us, but often lies dormant. "Only engagement can produce mastery," Pink explains (109).
- **Purpose** is a growing desire in today's workforce, exhibited by Baby Boomers and Millennials alike. Workers want to feel connected to a larger purpose and mission. They want to feel as if their work has meaning and as if what they do matters.

As Pink says (223), "Within organizations, people need to have purpose: In goals that use profit to reach purpose; in words that emphasize more than self-interest; and in policies that allow people to pursue purpose on their own terms."

Cafeteria Learning supports each of Pink's elements of intrinsic human motivation: When learners are in charge of their own learning and have the freedom to make their own choices (that is, experiencing a greater sense of **autonomy**), it means that not only can they do their jobs better (gaining competency and moving toward **mastery**), but they also have the opportunity to discover the intimate connection between their every-day tasks and the company's larger sense of purpose, mission, and values (fostering a deeper sense of **purpose**). This makes for a rich and satisfying workplace environment that benefits learners.

Cafeteria Learning is designed to grab learners' attention from the moment they enter the workshop and continue throughout the learning experience. As learners decide for themselves the activities to explore, their sense of autonomy builds along with their level of engagement with the content. The environment is set to develop mastery and purpose—learners make their own, meaningful connections to the content in real, purposeful ways.

> "[Cafeteria Learning] is about finding the knowledge inside of you, asking your peers, and working together."–*Cafeteria Learning workshop participant*

## Benefits to the Organization

In the article "Great Employees Make a Great Business," Michelle Nichols (2006) writes, "Which people are more valuable—good employees or good customers? While some might think this is a rhetorical 'chicken-or-egg' question, it isn't. The answer is—envelope please—good employees. This may surprise you . . . but a successful business starts with good employees who then attract good customers, not the other way around."

If the benefits of Cafeteria Learning to learners are great, wouldn't the benefits to the organization be equally great?

"This approach is exciting and engages individuals at all levels and functional areas of the company. It has been very well received in our retail environment where learners are used to being active and involved with others on the job. The autonomy this type of learning environment provides is appealing to our diverse workforce and takes into account differences in knowledge, experience, and educational background."–*Director of staffing and development*

Think of it this way: What kind of employees do you want to attract and retain in your organization—those who are intrinsically motivated toward performance and achievement, or those who need to be nudged, poked, and prodded to do their jobs?

With this in mind, it makes business sense to cultivate a company culture that attracts, supports, and encourages those who are self-motivated toward mastery and achievement. If you do this well, talented workers will flock to your organization. And cultivating the type of culture and environment that attracts and retains truly engaged employees begins with learning.

As part of its *State of the Global Workforce,* released in 2013, the Gallup Organization asked more than 25 million employees 12 questions, forming the Gallup Q12, a measure of employee engagement. One of these questions is: "At work, do you have the opportunity to do what you do best every day?" Learning professionals can take this one step further and ask the employees they're creating learning for: "At work, do you have the opportunity to learn the way you learn best?"

Cafeteria Learning leverages both intrinsic motivation and individualization. Participants often report aha moments that were never anticipated because they're learning from one another, and not just from the sage on the stage. By providing opportunities for employees to do what they do best and learn from one another, businesses can develop good employees who attract good customers.

## Benefits to the Learning Professional

Having spent more than a combined 40 years in the learning and development industry, we've heard many stories about learning professionals who were ready to pack their bags and call it quits. A friend of ours was one such person. She had grown tired of presenting information that inevitably fell on deaf ears, trying and failing to get through to learners who squirmed in their seats for hours on end, and knowingly perpetuating painfully ineffective training methods simply because "that's the way we've always done things." She had grown tired of the high tolerance for cutting corners and putting the benefit of stakeholders before learners. What was the point of staying in her job if she was only perpetuating frustration for the learners and herself?

"I was seriously considering switching careers," she said. "That is, until things began to change." Mind you, it wasn't as if her environment shifted, at least not at first: She was motivated to change her perspective, which in turn changed her belief in herself. She started to realize that things didn't have to be the way they were and that she actually had the power to make a real impact with her work. Bit by bit, she developed the courage to pitch active learning activities to stakeholders and implement them into her curriculum programs—and from that point on, her experience at work began to transform. Today, she is the curriculum development manager at a large organization, and her sense of passion, purpose, and ambition for her job and the industry at large is contagious.

Imagine the benefits you can experience when you make this kind of a shift, too: Instead of perhaps grumbling, learners will actually look forward to coming to your workshops. You'll see their faces light up at the sight of your interactive learning stations, as they share and engage with one another, and as they make meaningful connections between the content and their jobs. You'll delight in knowing that the learning experiences that you implement produce tangible, measurable organizational results (and so will management). And you'll begin to feel accomplished, empowered, and congruent in your role rather than stale, dissatisfied, and stuck.

# Can Cafeteria Learning Really Work for Your Organization?

We often meet learning professionals who are excited about Cafeteria Learning and other progressive approaches, yet they confide in us that they just haven't been able to make the switch.

"The thought of it gets me all jazzed up," said one industry peer. "But you know, it could never work in our organization."

She presented a couple of reasons why her organization must be different from other companies who've successfully implemented the approach:

- "Our stakeholders would never buy into this. They're so stuck on doing things the way they've always been done."
- "I catch our learners staring out the window during compliance training. . . . I just don't think it'll work for them."

Well, this actually makes them no different from anyone else. Contrary to what you might think, many of the companies and individuals who implement Cafeteria Learning faced these same questions, doubts, and challenges. Many of them worked for risk-averse organizations in which traditional training practices were not only accepted, but expected, and where management followed tradition like a script. Some operated as one-person training departments for their companies and faced obvious constraints in both budget and time. Many wondered how their learners would take to the new approach.

What's more, before implementing Cafeteria Learning, most of these learning professionals hadn't thought of themselves as particularly bold, risky, or progressive. Sure, they wanted to make changes and lead their learners in a new direction, but they weren't necessarily used to stepping outside their comfort zones or proposing new ideas. Doing so felt a little unnerving.

It doesn't take a big budget to make Cafeteria Learning work for your company. It doesn't take a Herculean effort, either. Consider this chapter the ultimate guide to socializing Cafeteria Learning into your organizational culture and attracting unwavering support from stakeholders— even if you think you don't have the time or resources to make it happen.

"Cafeteria Learning takes you back to the days when learning was fun and exciting. There's individual reflection, paired discussion, some game techniques, and the overarching choice which makes you the master of your learning. I didn't want it to end! Every learning professional should know about Cafeteria Learning and how to rekindle the excitement of learning in a business environment while meeting clear performance objectives."–*Cafeteria Learning workshop participant*

Consider these responses to the two reasons mentioned for why Cafeteria Learning couldn't work in your organization.

## "Stakeholders Would Never Buy Into This"

It can be difficult to implement new ways of doing things into your organization. Your stakeholders are so dead set on doing things the way they've always been done. You're sure that they'd never even consider implementing something like Cafeteria Learning. It's far too progressive, too different. It's just not their style.

These beliefs are understandable. If leadership has always done things a certain way, what reason is there to believe they'd be willing to do things any differently?

In reality, however, it can be easier than you'd think to get leadership on board with—and even excited about—something new. It just takes an understanding of how best to present the idea.

A great example comes from a manager of training and development for a large service corporation. Of the several companies she'd worked for in the past, she told us, her current company was the most conservative. Nevertheless, she'd managed to get executive leadership not just tentatively on board, but fully behind her Cafeteria Learning efforts.

And her story is not unique.

How did she do it? Despite their initial skepticism of the idea, she secured the stakeholders' support by speaking their language, starting small, and presenting the idea as an experiment:

## Speak the Stakeholders' Language

Imagine coming up with a plan that could increase achievement and desired results, and have a meaningful impact on the company's bottom line. But when you present the plan to the stakeholders, they stare back at you and say, "Sorry, we're not interested." Would this ever happen?

The mistake most people make when presenting new ideas is that they focus too much on matter-of-fact details, such as logistics and the nuts-and-bolts of how the program works, at the expense of what stakeholders actually care about most—results and tangible benefits to the organization.

Learn to speak in terms of the benefits Cafeteria Learning will bring to the organization (for example, increased engagement and effectiveness, and higher return on investment) and you'll have the stakeholders nodding "yes" before you know it.

## Start Small

Imagine that a few people come to your door one day with an unusual request: They want to place a large, ugly sign in your yard that reads, "Drive Carefully."

"We work for a nonprofit that promotes safe driving," they tell you.

If you're anything like us, you'd probably laugh loudly in their faces and exclaim, "Fat chance!" You're not alone. When Jonathan Freedman and Scott Fraser (1966) carried out such an experiment, only 17 percent of people said "yes" to the request.

If someone were to ring your doorbell and ask to place a small "Drive Carefully" sticker on your window, however, you'd be more likely to comply. In fact, when they asked a second group of homeowners to do so, virtually all of them agreed to the request.

The same applies when presenting new ideas to stakeholders. It's easy to say "no" to large requests, but often equally easy to say "yes" to small ones, so don't be afraid to start small. Instead of asking to roll out Cafeteria Learning company-wide, begin by asking to roll it out as a pilot for one department or group. Instead of presenting it as a huge overhaul of your existing methods, present it as one small piece of a blended approach that can help stakeholders become more comfortable over time. In his book *Revolutionize Learning & Development* (2014), Clark Quinn advises readers not to try and "boil the ocean."

We agree. Not only is this a reasonable approach for getting your foot in the door, but starting small also sets the stage for incorporating bigger changes over time. When Freedman and Fraser went back to the "window sticker" group a few weeks later and asked if they'd be willing to put the large, ugly signs in their yard, they found that this time an incredible 76 percent of homeowners said "yes."

What researchers call the "foot in the door technique" may be applied to requests to achieve higher compliance (Burger 1999). With the right attitude toward a reasonable request, people are not only more likely to say "yes" to a small request than a large one, but they are also more likely to say "yes" to a larger request down the line if they've already agreed to a smaller one (Ahluwalia and Burnkrant 1993). Sweeping change doesn't often happen all at once; instead, it starts small and builds from there.

## Present It as an Experiment

"Let's just try it once and see what happens."

These are the kind of words that might have gotten you into trouble in high school, but they can actually be beneficial in the context of introducing more progressive approaches into a traditional organization.

Much the same as starting small helps scale down the risk factor in the eyes of the stakeholders, presenting it as an experiment helps remove even more risk. Stakeholders don't have to commit to Cafeteria Learning for the rest of their lives; they don't even have to commit for every quarter of the next fiscal year. They just have to be willing to let you try it out once and see what happens.

This is where proper evaluation becomes key. The proof is in the pudding, so be sure to provide leadership with a measurement plan ahead of time and an evaluation report after the trial run so they can see the results for themselves, including quantitative before-and-after measurements of the intended performance outcomes (see chapter 8). A colleague noted that leaders were fully on board and wanted to continue and expand upon the "experiment" once they saw the positive feedback and results.

So there you have it: three effective methods for getting your stakeholders on board with Cafeteria Learning or any other progressive learning approach. Getting management to buy into a new approach might seem like a difficult task to accomplish, but like many of the clients we've worked with, you'll be surprised at how easy it can be once you actually utilize these suggestions. Most of the time, the biggest impediment is simply your waiting to ask to try new approaches.

## "I Don't Think It Will Work for Learners"

You might be concerned that your learners will be unresponsive or reluctant and that getting them engaged in the process will be too difficult. Sure, it can take some learners a bit of time to ease into a more active form of learning, but can you blame them? After all, they've been conditioned from an early age to sit back in their chairs and be spoon-fed information.

That said, even the most timid and reluctant learners have gone from closed off and hesitant to open and engaged in a Cafeteria Learning session. By the end of the workshop, the participant who cautiously started off with a solo activity might be laughing and smiling with several of his colleagues as they play a board game together. The participant who entered the room reluctantly with hands in pockets might now be intent on building the perfect building block structure to demonstrate her perspective on the topic at hand. The magic of Cafeteria Learning is that there's something for everyone. By giving learners a choice in activities, they don't feel put on the spot or forced to participate in any one activity. As learners complete activities, they can choose to do so independently, in a pair, or with a small group. Cafeteria Learning removes the fear of "being called on" to provide the correct answer in front of the class.

People are innately curious and driven to learn, and giving them autonomy helps unlock this innate desire. Learners who might appear disengaged in one setting can suddenly become engaged and engrossed when placed in an environment that supports their learning needs.

Let's take a look at the approach a major retailer took to gain acceptance for Cafeteria Learning in a conservative culture.

In 2013, the client's training and development department was in the process of developing a brand-new development program for an audience of managers whom they hadn't provided structured training for in the past. The overarching goals of their program were threefold:

1. Ensure supervisors and managers had the skills needed to grow their staff.
2. Prepare supervisors and managers for future opportunities.
3. Demonstrate commitment to the management team through investment in training them.

In partnership with a group of senior leaders, their learning and development team had the vision to create a blended learning approach that included several weeks of self-study through online courses, followed by a workshop component that helped learners take the basic principles and concepts they'd learned online and apply them to their specific workplace situations.

"We didn't want to just hand our managers a generic training and say, 'Translate it yourself as to how it applies to your job'; we wanted to help them make that translation," said the training and development manager. "How could we take the concepts that were being taught in the online learning and then customize them for our particular audience?"

Based on their goals for the new program, a Cafeteria Learning–based approach was proposed that would help learners demonstrate the concepts they'd learned online in an interactive, customized way.

"It was a different type of approach than I had seen used before, but immediately we were very interested in it because we wanted the focus of our workshops to be interactive," said the training and development manager. "We wanted them to be as practical and as hands-on as we could get them, because the first piece of our program involved self-study, sitting at your desk, and having somebody talk at you. We really wanted people to be able to leave the workshop and do something different. We wanted to give them skills, not just impart information."

As the new program kicked off, she observed that while some learners were initially timid and unsure what to expect, they quickly grew comfortable with the approach and began stepping outside their comfort zones.

"People started off by gravitating toward the way of learning that they're most comfortable with," she explained. "And what we found is that over time, as we kept going back to Cafeteria Learning over and over again, people who originally gravitated toward one type of learning became increasingly brave. They would start off timid and wouldn't go to a station where they had to talk to somebody else, but by the time they had done it a couple of times, that's where the biggest learning occurred, and that's where people started to go because they felt more comfortable and confident that it was a safe place, and they could be wrong and it would be OK."

Feedback from learners was overwhelmingly positive. "I had people who came up to me the day after the first workshop and said, 'I did not want to come, I can't tell you what a relief it was because it was fun!' So people enjoyed it and they learned something. It's a very approachable and easy approach for people who might not be comfortable in a formal learning situation," she recounted.

Unprompted, several learners even sent her emails praising the workshop and its delivery:

- "Nice job . . . I look forward to more workshops with a similar structure."
- "Everyone was excited and impressed. The collaborative approach was a hit and the topics were very thought provoking."
- "I really appreciated the 'no pressure' approach. It was really a comfortable setting and I think you get the most out of people when they don't feel put on the spot."
- "I like the fact that there's really a focus on people exploring and finding the answers themselves as opposed to you feeding them the information."

## Summary

Getting approval to implement Cafeteria Learning in your organization begins with understanding the benefits to the learner, organization, and learning professional. Learners benefit as they learn in ways that meaningfully influence their work; experience autonomy, mastery, and purpose; and build new relationships with colleagues. Organizations benefit by attracting and retaining top performers who are intrinsically motivated toward performance and achievement, which inherently improves the company's levels of production and employee retention. Learning professionals benefit as they begin to have a meaningful impact on learners and the organization, increasing their feelings of accomplishment and satisfaction.

But to see these benefits, you first need to attain buy-in from stakeholders. Recommended best practices for securing stakeholder support include speaking the stakeholders' language in terms of benefits to the organization; starting with small requests for change as opposed to large, sweeping changes; and presenting a new learning approach as a temporary experiment rather than a permanent change.

Doubting that your learners will engage with a Cafeteria Learning approach, lacking the time or budget to implement a new approach, or feeling uncomfortable with change are often poor excuses not to implement progressive learning approaches such as Cafeteria Learning. Because Cafeteria Learning offers a variety of ways to engage with content, learners readily take to it and become more comfortable with the progressive approach the more they are exposed to it. Lastly, if you want to make a meaningful impact within your organization, it's necessary to take risks and step outside your own comfort zone.

# 4

# WRITING CAFETERIA LEARNING OBJECTIVES

Just as with any learning experience, designing an effective Cafeteria Learning workshop begins with writing learning objectives. Before you can create activities or workshop content, you need to have the end in mind. If you don't consider what your learners should be able to demonstrate on the job after the workshop, it won't matter how you design your workshop.

Cafeteria Learning objectives are unique in that there are relatively few of them and the design is typically based around three core objectives. They are also designed specifically to allow for choice. Here are four quick steps for creating learning objectives for Cafeteria Learning. The steps may look familiar, but they incorporate suggestions for how to complete them with choice in mind.

## Clarify Content

Subject matter experts (SMEs) and learning professionals need each other. Each brings different strengths and information to a project. The learning design expert can build an innovative, beautiful framework, but without the content expert's contribution, the structure could easily crumble (Figure 4-1). In the end, we all have the same goal: a dynamic learning experience that captures the audience's attention and makes a meaningful difference.

## Figure 4-1. Learning Professionals and SMEs Need to Work Together

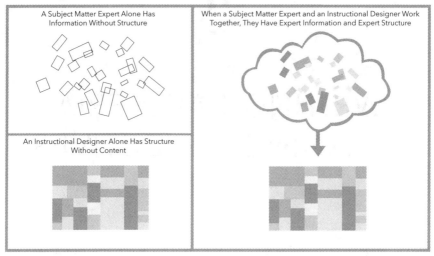

Some SMEs think learners should know everything possible about a given subject and thus would like to cram as much information into the learning program. They may be expressing their perceived need, or their stated request, typically a result of a problem they are experiencing. This is often phrased in terms of a preconceived solution they have already in mind. Instead, a well-designed learning experience should be limited to only the content that will achieve the desired goal. The process of writing effective and strategic learning objectives involves not only knowing what content to include, but nearly as important, what content not to include. This is why it's so essential when crafting your learning objectives to always begin with the end in mind.

By clarifying content, you'll be able to provide an effective structure for the vast amounts of information that you (or your SME) possess, crafting strategic learning objectives in the process. Here are some tips to remember when working with SMEs to clarify content:

- **Understand your role.** Learning professionals are not often experts in the content areas they write about, nor should they expect to become experts. Learn as much as possible about the subject to create a learning experience that's meaningful for the audience. The added expertise will enable you to organize and create a fabulous learning program.

- **It's mostly about respect.** Regard SMEs as the true experts. Sometimes they bring 30 years of detailed knowledge. Even if this knowledge comes in the form of a pile of printed materials thicker than the tallest coffee mug, still take the time to review the information the SME compiled. By building respect with the SME, you'll improve access to reliable resources that you'll need to accomplish your goals.
- **Guide the conversation.** Communicate the big picture for the learning program and ultimately design the course only using the content that supports the learning objectives. If multiple SMEs are involved and they're saying different things, actively listen to seek clarification and consistency.

## Identify the Learning Outcome

For the most part, training requests won't come to you as, "We need a Cafeteria Learning workshop." Instead, requests will likely sound like "we need sales training" or "we need diversity training" or "we need a conflict management workshop." However, these requests don't describe the desired outcome for the learning experience; they may provide a clue as to what the goal might be, but not the specific goal itself. If you receive these kinds of requests, dig deeper and uncover the specific learning outcome.

When identifying the learning outcome, think of it as the tangible, measurable benefit to the organization as a result of the learner's participation in the learning experience. For example, an outcome for a workshop on the science of learning might be to increase the use of brain-based learning principles when designing sales training.

## Identify the Learning Objectives

The next step is to determine the learning objectives that will contribute to the achievement of the goal. Learning objectives are the measurable results of the learners' participation in the learning activities, or stated another way, what the learners will be able to demonstrate as a result of what they have learned.

Aristotle once said, "For the things we have to learn before we can do them, we learn by doing them" (Bynum and Porter 2005). And David Kolb (1984) proposed that to gain knowledge from an experience, the learner must:

- Be willing to be actively involved in the experience.
- Be able to reflect on the experience.
- Possess and use analytical skills to conceptualize the experience.
- Possess decision-making and problem-solving skills to use the new ideas gained from the experience.

So when you begin writing learning objectives, you should determine what knowledge, skills, and attitudes learners will need to demonstrate the stated outcome. In our science of learning workshop example, a learning objective might look something like this: At the end of the workshop, learners will be able to explain three strategies to implement brain-based learning principles.

Of course, this is just one of the learning objectives necessary to achieve the outcome. What's important is that you can actually measure the learner's ability to explain three strategies to implement brain-based learning principles.

If your initial list consists of more than three learning objectives, the next step is to condense your list to just three around which your Cafeteria Learning workshop and activities will revolve. Over time, we've found that three learning objectives is the right number to deliver a two- to three-hour Cafeteria Learning workshop. If you have more than three learning objectives, the workshop can become chaotic; if you have less than three, there aren't enough choices, which affects the richness of the learner's experience. Barry Schwartz, author of *The Paradox of Choice: Why More Is Less* (2004), points out that while choice is critical to freedom and autonomy, too much choice can create a burden on the individual. With too many options, people tend to regret their original choice and become stressed or unhappy, wondering if they should have chosen a different option. That's why we like to stick with three activities per learning objective, which gives us nine activities. Any more than that and learners may become overwhelmed with choices, thus detracting from the learning experience.

## Allow for Choice

Informal learning expert Jay Cross (2007) wrote, "Training is something that's imposed on you; learning is something you choose. Knowledge workers thrive when given the freedom to decide how they will do what's asked of them." Cross couldn't be more right.

Writing learning objectives for a Cafeteria Learning workshop should allow for choice in learning. They should be written in such a way that you will be able to design three different activities for each objective. Regardless of what activity the learners choose, they all should be able to reach the same learning objective.

This is the beauty of Cafeteria Learning—learners have a choice of activities to participate in rather than only having to experience the one activity that has been provided to them. By its very nature, Cafeteria Learning leaves the *how* to learn the content up to the learner. Learners can construct their own knowledge in an exploratory and self-directed manner, one in which they're free to choose their own unique learning paths within a defined framework aligned with the learning objectives.

We put our theory—if learning objectives are written to allow for choice, learners should be able to reach the same learning objective regardless of the activity they choose—to the test during a Cafeteria Learning workshop we were teaching for talent development professionals. During this workshop we intentionally did not communicate the learning objectives and instead asked learners to reflect on what they'd learned as a result of attending the workshop. We then asked them to write what they believed the learning objectives were based on their experience. After reviewing everyone's lists as a group, learners agreed that they had all reached the same core learning objectives (Table 4-1). One learner, whose title was director of customer service learning and development, noted that "it was interesting to see that while everyone had the opportunity to learn differently, they were able to walk away with . . . the same learning objectives."

Table 4-1. Identified Objectives Closely Matched Actual Learning Objective

| Actual Learning Objective | Learner Identified Objectives |
|---|---|
| Describe three strategies to implement brain-based learning principles. | • Explore new options for delivering learning based on how the brain works.<br>• List the basic principles of brain-based learning.<br>• Apply best practices to enhance experiential learning. |

A well-designed Cafeteria Learning workshop creates a learning environment in which all learners reach a similar destination regardless of the path they take; writing learning objectives that allow for choice will help you on your way to creating that environment.

## Summary

Choice is the component that most distinguishes Cafeteria Learning from lecture-based learning models and enhances the learning process. When designing a Cafeteria Learning experience, clarify the content and identify the desired outcome for the learners, as you would with any learning program. The next step is unique to Cafeteria Learning: Identify your learning objectives and ensure they allow for choice. If you miss this critical step, you may find it challenging to design the three activities to support each learning objective. (We'll review designing activities and how to enhance choice for learners in the next chapter.)

The Revised Bloom's Taxonomy is a great resource for ideas when writing learning objectives for choice. For example, "Summarize limitations of lecture-based learning" is too restrictive; it implies that the only way to reach the desired objective is through summarization, when that is just one way to demonstrate an understanding of the limitations of lecture-based learning. A better way to phrase this objective might be, "Identify 10 limitations of lecture-based learning." This allows for a number of options by which to achieve the same outcome.

# 5

# DESIGNING CAFETERIA LEARNING ACTIVITIES

Once you've determined your learning objectives, the next step is to design the activities that will help your learners reach them. Chapter 10 offers a selection of our most popular Cafeteria Learning activities presented in a template so you can fill them in with your own content. Of course, once you are more familiar with the process you are probably going to want to design your own activities. Let's take a look at how to do that.

## Brainstorm Activities

In the fall of 2015, we conducted a workshop for our local ATD chapter in which we walked through the science of learning theory that supports the Cafeteria Learning method, had learners participate in a Cafeteria Learning workshop, and then had them design their own activities. The workshop was a big hit; however, it became clear that learners found it difficult to brainstorm activities. It takes experience, creativity, time, and practice to design learning this way.

What you'll want to do first is schedule a brainstorming session. If it's just you, don't skip over brainstorming entirely. You can still do it even if you're going solo. Here are a few tips:

- Get outside, talk with other people, look for inspiring images, and read anything you can get your hands on that's not about the content you're working with.

- While it may seem obvious, make sure you dedicate time to brainstorming—whether for a few minutes each day or one large chunk of time, you're going to need time.
- Don't dismiss any of your ideas outright—if you find yourself judging your ideas, clear your mind and continue to come up with the most ideas you can. All ideas are welcome.
- If you need a little more structure, creating mind maps serves as a wonderful tool when it's just you brainstorming.
- Try distancing yourself from technology in your creative space, including silencing your devices. This will go far in ensuring that the time you've set aside for brainstorming doesn't get interrupted.

If you're fortunate to have others available to brainstorm with you, schedule a brainstorming session. Set the stage for the experience to be highly creative, fast paced, and engaging. Be sure to welcome and document all ideas, and don't qualify ideas yet. Remember, you want quantity, not quality. You will whittle them down later.

To begin the brainstorming session, review each learning objective one at a time and think about all the different ways each could be achieved. You could silently brainstorm for a few minutes with each team member writing one idea on a sticky note and then putting it up on a whiteboard or wall.

When brainstorming, think about your favorite board games, video games, apps, K-12 classroom experiences, and so forth. Also review any past activities you've had success with and could repurpose.

Once you have enough ideas to work with, have each team member explain his inspiration for his ideas while the rest ask questions and build on one another's thoughts. Through this process, you might even come up with completely new ideas. Some of the best ideas are activities that evolve from the brainstorm but weren't actually one of the original ideas. Sometimes ideas come easily; other times the process takes many brainstorming sessions. Even if you thought you had an amazing activity that ultimately fell flat with learners, keep tinkering with it: The effort will be worth your time in the end.

We put our brainstorming skills to the test and came up with a workshop about brain-based learning (Table 5-1).

Table 5-1. Brainstorm Activities Example

Explain one or more benefits of brain-based learning.

- Individually or with a partner, review principles of brain-based learning. (Conversation cards have a fact on one side and a related discussion prompt on the other side.)
- With a partner or in a small group, choose from a list of brain-based learning techniques and identify the benefits.
- With a partner, find out how priming helps prepare our brain for learning. (Several priming exercises are available to experience first-hand how priming works).

# Check Activities Against Learning Experience Categories

To ensure that you provide an adequate range of choices for your learners, you'll want to check that the activities you've brainstormed reflect a variety of learning experiences. You can organize them across three categories:

1. learning preference
2. interaction
3. technology.

Tables 5-2, 5-3, and 5-4 describe each of these learning experience categories.

## Learning Preference

Note we intentionally use the term *learning preference* here, not *learning style*. As discussed in chapter 1, learning styles are widely believed to be an inappropriate determinant for how you structure a learning offering. Instead, people learn in many ways, although they do tend to have preferences for how they learn. Cafeteria Learning does not presume to match the learning preference to the individual, but rather allows individuals to choose the way they prefer to learn at that particular moment in time.

Sometimes an extrovert feels introspective, and sometimes an introvert wants to talk things through. It's nice to have a choice.

You certainly could argue that any one activity can reflect many learning preferences; for example, connecting a chain of paper clips includes both visual and kinesthetic properties. However, when creating Cafeteria Learning activities, you should aim to identify the *primary* learning preference the activity supports. This will help you provide a range of activities that support the various learning preferences.

Let's review each of these learning preferences in a little more detail (Table 5-2).

Table 5-2. Category 1: Learning Preference

| Learning Preference | What It Looks Like in Cafeteria Learning |
|---|---|
| Problem solving | An activity that requires learners to solve a real-world or simulated problem. |
| Competitive | An activity in which individuals or teams compete against each other to achieve an objective. |
| Collaborative | An activity in which individuals or teams collaborate with each other to achieve an objective. |
| Visual | An activity that's specifically designed to help learners learn in a way that is primarily visual. |
| Auditory | An activity that's specifically designed to help learners learn in a way that is primarily auditory. |
| Kinesthetic | An activity that requires that learners use part of the body (for example, hands, actions, and expressions) to create or do something. |
| Reflective | An inward reflection of one's past experience, such as recalling a memory or interpreting an emotional response. |

Problem solving gives learners the choice to solve a real-world or simulated problem. With problem solving, or problem-based learning, learners think strategically to solve a carefully crafted, open-ended problem and learn from success and failure in a safe environment. This type of activity can be used with individuals, with pairs, or in a group.

The use of competition in learning can work well if an activity is created to be balanced and fair. A competitive activity may motivate learners to excel and achieve the objective, while also creating a different level of excitement in the workshop. Learners can reflect on their own strengths and weaknesses and learn what to do to improve themselves.

Collaborative, or cooperative, learning brings learners together in an activity with opportunities to reflect upon and reply to diverse points of view and responses. As learners work to achieve the objective, a variety of input combines their range of perspectives into a more complete and comprehensive result.

Visual, auditory, or kinesthetic learning comes from the 1920s' classification by psychologists of the most common ways that people learn. However, in practice, people tend to mix and match these three styles, rather than adhere strictly to one alone.

Sometimes learners like to take time to examine their thoughts and reactions; a reflective activity is a great way to provide this option. This kind of activity can increase self-awareness as learners make a conscious effort to think about the content.

## Interaction

By giving learners the choice over whether they'd like to participate in an activity with others—with a partner or with a larger group—or by themselves, you allow them to match their comfort with the learning process (Table 5-3). Going further, you can sometimes offer an activity that can encompass multiple interaction types with only slight modifications. This makes the activity even more powerful because it can then appeal to designers wishing to provide more options for interaction to the learners.

## Technology

Despite the proliferation of technology in people's work and personal lives, individuals still have differing degrees of comfort with its operation (Table 5-4). If you only provide activities that require more advanced technological abilities, participants who are unaccustomed to using tablets might find themselves at a disadvantage and ultimately fail to learn. However, technology provides wonderful opportunities to connect learners to the content and to each other; totally ignoring technology would be a fool's errand.

Table 5-3. Category 2: Interaction

| Interaction | What It Looks Like in Cafeteria Learning |
|---|---|
| Individual | Completing activities individually may appeal to learners who seek independence in, and ownership of, their learning. Successfully completing learning alone can result in increased motivation and confidence in their mastery of content as well. |
| Partner | Partnership learning may result in learners becoming more actively, and visibly, engaged in an activity. The material in partner-based activities can foster a more interesting and rich experience with learners sharing knowledge unique to them. |
| Group | Like learning with a partner, learning in a group setting brings at least three learners together to reflect upon and reply to the diverse points of view each brings to the group learning experience. |

Table 5-4. Category 3: Technology

| Technology | What It Looks Like in Cafeteria Learning |
|---|---|
| High tech | An activity that makes use of modern technology. Depending on the availability of technology, designers can build wildly creative learning experiences for learners. With access to the Internet, learners can be connected to information quickly—and activities can be based around researching or gaming. |
| Low tech | A low-tech activity is simply one that doesn't use technology. |

An example of a high-tech activity is to provide a discussion prompt for learners to answer on camera. Most tablets and laptops have a built-in function for this. Some learners love the opportunity to share their perspective; it allows them to reflect and share, and in doing so they are processing the content in a really powerful way. Others think this activity sounds like a nightmare. That's what is so great about what Cafeteria Learning provides. The more reticent learner can still benefit by sitting down and watching the stories recorded by others. It is a simple but powerful experience that is so much more effective than asking people to put ideas on a flipchart. Learners could have a similar experience with just an audio recording. (The StoryCorps project that airs on NPR is an example of an emotionally engaging audio experience. Its mission is to provide people of all backgrounds and beliefs with the opportunity to record, share, and preserve the stories of our lives.)

Table 5-5 offers an example of how you would check your activities against the learning experience categories. This exercise helps you ensure that the activities represent a variety of learning experiences, allowing adequate choice for the learner. All options in each category related to the activity are selected in this example for illustrative purposes. Another technique is to select only the *primary* learning preference, interaction type, and technology type.

## Select Final Activities

After brainstorming a comprehensive list of activities and checking the activities against the learning experience categories, the next step is to narrow your list to three activities for each learning objective. After this step is completed, you'll have nine total activities for your Cafeteria Learning workshop.

As you consider which activities to keep and which to discard, you'll want to ensure that you have a balance of learning preferences, interaction types, and technology types. You do not want all your activities to be completed in small groups, because that prevents those who prefer to work alone from having the option to do so. Likewise, learners may prefer to steer away from technology-based activities, while others may be drawn to it.

Chapter 5

Table 5-5. Check Activities Against Learning Experience Categories Example

| Learning Objective 1: Explain 3 Strategies to Implement Brain-Based Learning Principles | | | |
|---|---|---|---|
| Individually or with a partner, review principles of brain-based learning. (Conversation cards have a fact on one side and a related discussion prompt on the other side.) | **Learning Preference**<br>☐ problem solving<br>☐ competitive<br>☒ collaborative<br>☐ visual<br>☐ auditory<br>☐ kinesthetic<br>☐ reflective | **Interaction**<br>☒ individual<br>☒ partner<br>☐ group | **Technology**<br>☐ high tech<br>☒ low tech |
| With a partner or in a small group, choose from a list of brain-based learning techniques and identify the benefits. | **Learning Preference**<br>☐ problem solving<br>☐ competitive<br>☒ collaborative<br>☐ visual<br>☐ auditory<br>☐ kinesthetic<br>☒ reflective | **Interaction**<br>☐ individual<br>☒ partner<br>☒ group | **Technology**<br>☐ high tech<br>☒ low tech |
| With a partner, find out how priming helps prepare our brain for learning. (Several priming exercises are available to experience firsthand how priming works.) | **Learning Preference**<br>☐ problem solving<br>☐ competitive<br>☒ collaborative<br>☐ visual<br>☐ auditory<br>☒ kinesthetic<br>☐ reflective | **Interaction**<br>☐ individual<br>☒ partner<br>☐ group | **Technology**<br>☐ high tech<br>☒ low tech |

# Plan and Document Activity Details

Once you've selected your nine final activities, the last step in designing Cafeteria Learning activities is to plan and document the details of each activity. To simplify the planning and documentation process, we've developed a design document as shown in Figures 5-1a and 5-1b. Check out chapter 10 for examples of completed design documents for sample activities.

Some of the activity details, such as the topic title, activity title, foundational content, activity instructions, and reflection questions, will eventually be used to populate the instructions that you'll place at each activity station for learners to reference. The learning objective, activity description, and learning experience categories are for your own reference and documentation. Activity details such as the estimated time and materials are documented for planning purposes. This enables you to plan the amount of time learners may need for each activity, as well as the materials you'll need to purchase or create for each activity.

Planning and documenting activity details in one document provides an easy way to keep track of everything related to the activity. With so many moving parts—preparing for and setting up all the materials for nine activities, plus the primer, foundational content, and debrief—it's important to plan and document. Let's take a look at each component of the Cafeteria Learning design document in detail.

## Topic Title

Determine a topic title that succinctly captures the outcome of the activity's learning objective. The topic title helps you, as well as the learner, quickly identify which topic each activity belongs to—without having to write out the full learning objective.

## Learning Objective

Document the learning objective this activity is aligned with. It's important to keep this in front of you so you can verify that your activity meets the learning objective.

Figure 5-1a. Cafeteria Learning Design Document (front)

| Topic Title | Learning Objective | |
|---|---|---|
| **Topic Overview** | | |

| Activity Title | | Estimated Time |
|---|---|---|

| **Learning Preference** | | | **Interaction** | | **Technology** |
|---|---|---|---|---|---|
| ☐ Problem Solving | ☐ Collaboration | ☐ Auditory | ☐ Reflective | ☐ Individual | ☐ Group | ☐ High Tech |
| ☐ Competition | ☐ Visual | ☐ Kinesthetic | | ☐ Partner | | ☐ Low Tech |

**Activity Instructions**

1.

2.

3.

Figure 5-1b. Cafeteria Learning Design Document (back)

| Topic Debrief | | | |
|---|---|---|---|

| Produce | Purchase | Workshop Materials | | | | | | |
|---|---|---|---|---|---|---|---|---|
| | | | | | | | | |
| | | | | | | | | |
| | | | | | | | | |
| | | | | | | | | |
| | | | | | | | | |
| | | | | | | | | |

## Foundational Content

For each of the three activities that support a single learning objective, provide some background information. This is one place in which you might provide some of the information that you'd normally tell learners in a typical lecture-style workshop. Ideally this is no more than a few paragraphs. Ultimately this foundational content will end up on your activity instruction cards.

## Activity Title

Give your activity a memorable title, which will be visible to learners on the instruction card placed at each activity station. A catchy title is intended to pique learner curiosity and interest in participating in the activity. This will appear on the activity menu under each activity title to help learners decide which activity they want to choose.

## Activity Description

Write one to two sentences that summarize the way learners will engage in the activity. In addition to the activity title, this will appear on the activity menu to help learners decide which activity they want to choose.

## Learning Experience Categories

Document the learning preference, interaction type, and technology type of each activity. Although you've already determined the learning experience categories for each of your activities, the goal at this point is to document it for easy reference.

## Estimated Time

Consider the estimated length of time the activity should take. We find that many of our activities take about 10-15 minutes to finish. Each of your activities should be designed to take approximately the same amount of time to complete. At this point, until the workshop is implemented, these are only estimates. To ensure all activities wrap up at about the same time, make sure to give learners notification when there is 15 minutes left to complete the activity portion of the workshop. This will allow them to self-assess and determine how many activities they need to complete to get to the "at least one from each topic" requirement. If learners finish the requirement with time to spare, remind them that they can complete additional activities.

## Materials

Document the necessary materials for each activity, including whether you'll need to purchase them or produce them yourself. This is another aspect of planning: By writing down details such as the source and price for items you plan to purchase, you can save time preparing for the workshop. Research the materials you need to purchase so you know how long it will take to receive them before the workshop. If you can create the material yourself, you'll be better able to determine how much time you need to design, develop, and produce.

## Activity Instructions

Craft a set of step-by-step instructions for each activity, which will eventually be used to populate the instruction cards that you'll place at each activity station for learners to reference. When writing instructions be succinct; extra words can sometimes confuse rather than clarify. Cafeteria Learning activities are self-directed, so activity instructions need to be written in such a way as to ensure each learner completes the activity following the same steps each time.

## Reflection Questions

Once learners have completed the activity, give them an opportunity to reflect on their experience and perhaps discuss it with others. We like to include the activity reflection questions on the instruction cards learners see at each activity station (see the "Discuss" column in Figure 5-3).

# Prepare Workshop Materials

The activities are just one portion of a Cafeteria Learning workshop, so it's important to prepare for the other parts, too. Chapter 6 focuses on the structure to help you create a successful workshop. Preparing the workshop agenda, activity menu, and instruction cards brings you one step closer.

## Workshop Agenda

Build an agenda for the learning experience that ensures everything is covered and the experience stays on track. Here's how a typical Cafeteria Learning workshop is organized:

1. A brief welcome and introduction.
2. A priming activity and corresponding debrief.
3. Delivery of foundational content by facilitator.
4. A brief description of what Cafeteria Learning is and how it works. When introducing Cafeteria Learning to your learners, make sure to touch on the following items:
   ◦ Let them know that Cafeteria Learning is designed to give them the freedom to choose how they learn, and that like a cafeteria, stations are set up around the room to offer them choices.
   ◦ Ask them to browse the activity menu and to choose at least one activity from each topic on the menu.
   ◦ Let them know that it's not necessary to do all the activities; each activity has been designed to help them learn the same content, no matter how they choose to learn.
5. An overview of each of the available activities. Before turning learners loose to explore, show them where each activity is located around the room and give them a brief overview of the instructions for each one. Also let them know that written instructions are included at each station for their reference, and that you will be available during activities to answer their questions.
6. Activities. The time you set aside for learners to explore and choose among activities should be the largest block of time on your agenda.
7. A debriefing activity.

## Activity Menu

An activity menu (Figure 5-2) is an at-a-glance reference for learners to have throughout the activity portion of the workshop. The menu can be designed in various ways, but the key is to keep it simple and easy to interpret.

In place of a participant guide, learners refer to their activity menu when choosing activities. We've found that color-coding each topic on the menu to correspond with color-coded signs or flags at each activity station helps learners navigate the learning environment. Checkboxes next to the description of each activity help learners quickly see the activities they have completed. Defining space on the back of the menu is helpful for note-taking.

Figure 5-2. A Sample Activity Menu

## Applying the Science of Learning to Instructional Design

### Choose • Explore • Engage

Please Choose at Least One Activity From Each Topic Below. If Time Allows, You May Complete More.

| Limitations of Lecture | Brain-Based Learning | Best Practices |
|---|---|---|
| ☐ **A Picture Is Worth 1,000 Words**<br>Select the picture that best represents how you feel about lectures. | ☐ **Brain Cards**<br>Review principles of brain-based learning alone or with a partner. | ☐ **Chunking & Memory**<br>Compete with a partner and explore how categorizing content helps with retention. |
| ☐ **Trainers and Learners**<br>Use a flipchart to discover the limits of lecture. | ☐ **Small Group Discussion**<br>Choose from a list of techniques and discuss. | ☐ **Heads Up!**<br>Can you guess the words you're wearing based on the other player's clues? |
| ☐ **The Lamest Lesson**<br>Share your worst learning experience and listen to those of others. | ☐ **Priming the Brain**<br>Find out how priming helps prepare our brains for learning. | ☐ **Best Learning Memory**<br>Share your best learning experience and listen to those of others. |

## Instruction Cards

To prepare for your workshop, you'll need to create instruction cards for each activity station. We like to design our activity instruction cards with four distinct components, each of which you can pull from the design document you've already populated:

1.  topic title
2.  foundational content
3.  activity instructions
4.  reflection questions.

Figure 5-3. A Sample Instruction Card

**A Picture Is Worth 1,000 Words**

Select the picture that best represents how you feel about lectures.

| Overview | Instructions | Discuss |
|---|---|---|
| Lecture-based learning was developed 200 years ago at the dawn of the Industrial Revolution.<br><br>It's authorization by nature, not collaborative. Lectures assume that the teacher has the information and learners need to open up their thinking caps so the teacher can pour the information in. One of the main arguments levied against lecture is how little it truly engages students.<br><br>*"If keeping someone's attention in a lecture was a business it would have an 80% failure rate."*<br><br>—John Medina, *Brain Rules* | Choose an image that represents one of the following:<br><br>• a negative or ineffective learning experience you have had<br>• depicts the limitations of traditional classroom training<br>• sparks a new idea about how how you might be able to deliver training.<br><br>Finish the sentence on the card and leave it on the table for others to view.<br><br>If working with a partner, discuss the image you chose. | • What are some of the limitations of lecture?<br><br>• What are some of the conditions under which real learning can take place? |

## Summary

Designing a Cafeteria Learning workshop takes time, discipline, creativity, and a lot of planning. Weaving in the power of choice for learners requires learning professionals to flex their instructional design muscles. If you follow the design steps outlined in this chapter, you—and your learners—will be rewarded with a transformative learning experience that taps into active, social, and experiential learning and holds choice at its core. The next chapter shows you how to frame the activities to further optimize the learning experience.

# 6

# THE FRAMEWORK

While the foundation of Cafeteria Learning is the activities, a successful workshop also provides a solid framework to provide a complete learning experience. Like a great story, the workshop should contain three main parts: a beginning (appetizer), middle (the main course), and end (dessert). With Cafeteria Learning, the beginning is a priming activity that hooks learners' attention immediately, the middle is where learners explore content through the variety of self-directed activities, and the end is an opportunity to debrief the content, synthesize meaning, and prepare learners to apply the content on the job.

## Priming

A Cafeteria Learning workshop kicks off with priming, which serves to whet learners' appetites and gets them thinking about important topics before the workshop officially begins. In chapter 2, the benefits of priming were discussed, including increasing learners' abilities to retrieve information in the future and activating an important problem-solving area of the brain.

During the priming phase, learners begin by exploring terms and concepts at a high level. This helps them begin thinking about the content and referring to their own experiences and existing knowledge to help them build connections before the workshop officially begins. Priming helps the memory retrieve information when stimulated, causing a chain reaction in which one part of a concept is linked to another (Bodie, Powers, and Fitch-Hauser 2006, 125). It can affect decision making by preparing someone for a particular word, phrase, or idea. It's often used in advertising but can be used in learning when introducing new concepts.

## Example of Priming Activity

For the priming activity in the brain-based learning workshop, learners select one quote card from the poster as they enter the room. Each quote card has a fact or a thought-provoking quote about brain-based learning attached to it. For example, "All knowledge is connected to all other knowledge. The fun is in making the connections"—paleopathologist Arthur Aufderheide. Or "I am always doing that which I cannot do, in order that I may learn how to do it"—artist Pablo Picasso.

We then provided discussion questions for learners to answer based on the quote card they selected. For example, "What first came to mind when you read the quote card?" As learners await the official start of the workshop, their brains are already getting ready to learn.

# Foundational Content

Before launching into the main activities of your workshop, consider what knowledge or context you need to provide to ensure that your learners have a common baseline from which to partake in the main activities.

Foundational content should be brief (we recommend no more than 10 minutes) and commonly consists of definitions, related company policies, or a brief overview of the topic at hand. This portion of the workshop creates a nice transition from the priming activity. While the intention of priming is to get learners to think about the topic, the foundational content ensures that all the learners begin with the same knowledge. The lecture technique is employed, but only briefly so that learners have the opportunity to synthesize the information before their attention span begins to wane. In John Medina's *Brain Rules* (2008), the fourth rule reminds us, "We don't pay attention to boring things." So make sure this portion of the workshop is no more than 10 minutes. Medina writes (74), "What happens at the 10-minute mark to cause such trouble?

Nobody knows. The brain seems to be making choices according to some stubborn timing pattern, undoubtedly influenced by both culture and gene. This fact suggests a teaching and business imperative: Find a way to arouse and then hold somebody's attention for a specific period of time."

## Example of Foundational Content

A brief introduction to Medina's brain rules sets the stage for the learning to come. Two of the brain rules are discussed—the first rule states that exercise boosts brain power and the fifth that repetition is key to remembering—along with research data and examples.

# Debriefing

As is true with any learning effort, debriefing is a critical component of Cafeteria Learning. Learners have had a substantial chunk of time to engage in the activities of their choosing. Debriefing done well blends the immediate learning experience with real-work situations once learners leave the workshop space. For learners to apply what they learned, they must:

- See the value in applying it.
- Know how to apply it.
- Be given the opportunity to apply it (Wick et al. 2006).

In Cafeteria Learning, you have three opportunities to debrief learning. The first is to have reflection questions for learners at each activity station. These questions relate directly to the specific activity or topic and can be answered individually, in pairs, or in a small group, depending on the structure of the activity.

The second way is to debrief as a large group. When it's time to wrap up the activities, the facilitator brings all learners back together and summarizes the lessons learned for each of the three main topics. This is meant to be a high-level communication to validate that learners experienced similar outcomes and reached the learning objectives.

Debriefing usually involves asking questions that help learners organize, assimilate, and share what they've discovered throughout the workshop. A third way to debrief learning is to ask specific questions of each learner on what she learned. The facilitator either distributes note-cards to all learners with prepared questions and instructs them to take a few minutes to reflect and write down their responses or distributes blank notecards and asks questions aloud to the group. The facilitator then collects the completed notecards, and, one a time, reads them aloud and emphasizes the learning outcome.

Debriefing requires solid facilitation skills. The role of the facilitator is to guide the debriefing discussion. The goal here is to ensure that:

- There is effective participation.
- Learners achieve a mutual understanding.
- All contributions are considered and included in the ideas, solutions, or decisions that emerge.
- Learners take shared responsibility for the outcome.

We also like to get learners to think as much as possible about ways in which they can apply the workshop's content to their individual work-places or everyday lives. Asking learners to come up with a personal goal or takeaway related to the theme of the workshop is one way of doing this.

After learners have put their time and energy into the activities, the debriefing activity serves to tie it back to the learning objectives and enable learners to make connections between significant individual aha moments. For a skilled facilitator, the process of debriefing each learning topic should come quite naturally, although it is always a good invest-ment of time for a facilitator to prepare thoroughly before any workshop, including preparing for the debriefing.

Here are some best practices for debriefing Cafeteria Learning:

1. Debrief by topic. State the learning objective for each topic and describe the related activities.
2. Identify where learners have contributed time and energy to activities. Many times these are some of the larger wall-based or scribing activities. This can help inform your timing estimates and highlight which activities were popular.
3. Ask learners to share some of their thoughts on these activities.

4. If you get little feedback, read some of the activity responses from the wall charts to guide discussion.
5. Act on opportunities to tie the learners' experience back to the objectives for each topic.
6. Connect learners' comments.
7. Revisit the objectives and remind learners of each activity in the topic. Ask them if they believe they achieved the objective through their learning.

## Example of a Debriefing Activity

For the debriefing activity, you might pick one of the most popular activities from each topic and facilitate a group discussion around each one. Example questions include, "What was most surprising to you about that activity?" and "Did anyone else who participated in a different activity in this topic find something similar?" or "How did this activity help you think differently about the potential uses of brain-based learning?"

You don't always have to carefully plan the detail of the debriefing activity ahead of time—to a large extent, the particulars of a debriefing activity will be dictated by the experience of the group. An experienced facilitator will be able to follow the group's lead while simultaneously ensuring that he touches upon the main topics of the workshop, using his judgment to select debriefing activities and questions relevant to the particular group.

## Summary

If you are trying to create an effective environment for learning and provide a variety of activities (choices), but don't provide structure or a framework around activities, learners may feel lost, unable to focus. Without effective boundaries, learners will not be able to do what you need and want them to do because their brains can't work that way. The framework presented here for a Cafeteria Learning workshop allows learners to focus on a specific concept tied to the learning objective, removes distractions and excess information, and continuously stimulates learners with the necessary knowledge, just when they need it. By instilling a framework, through priming, foundational content, and debriefing, you are creating the right conditions to help learners be at their best, and when they're at their best, they thrive and positive results stream in.

# 7

# FACILITATING CAFETERIA LEARNING

While Cafeteria Learning might seem simple in theory, it involves quite a few moving pieces: What do you need to do to prepare for your workshop? How do you set up the room? How do you introduce learners to the concept of Cafeteria Learning? How does a typical workshop unfold?

What's more, facilitating a Cafeteria Learning workshop involves a shift in mindset regarding the role most learning professionals are used to taking. Rather than directly delivering content to learners, your role is to facilitate an experience in which learners can seek out and find the knowledge for themselves.

So what are the nuts and bolts of facilitating an amazing Cafeteria Learning experience? This chapter outlines the best practices for implementing a Cafeteria Learning workshop.

## Preparation Prior to the Workshop

Completing the following activities a month before the workshop gives you ample time to assemble the necessary materials and make any needed adjustments without causing too much stress. Facilitating any workshop is a big responsibility; with all the moving parts of a Cafeteria Learning workshop, give yourself enough time so you're confident everything is ready for your learners on the day of the workshop.

## Reserve a Workshop Location and Familiarize Yourself With It

When your Cafeteria Learning workshop is still a month away, go ahead and book the space you'll need. To the extent possible, become familiar with the learning environment. There may be times when you need lots of wall space for activities and find yourself in a room with a ton of windows, or in a room that's just too small. To avoid surprises like this, familiarize yourself with your reserved space in advance, giving yourself plenty of time to address any challenges. For cases in which wall space is sparse, you can bring in easels or tape to hang your mind maps, flip-charts, or other wall activities. You'll have time to figure out the logistics of bringing in more tables or chairs. Whatever the challenge, you can avoid the pressure of having to figure it out at the last minute.

## Purchase and Produce All Necessary Materials

Using your design document as a reference, purchase or produce all the necessary materials well in advance of your workshop. The workshop materials don't have to be fancy. You can write out instructions for each activity on a dry-erase board or a sheet of paper, hand-draw your game boards, and create just about anything you might need with nothing more than a word processor, a printer, and some markers. What matters most is that your materials are effective in helping learners reach their learning objectives, not necessarily the professional production of the materials.

## Practice Delivering the Content

You should practice delivering your introductory content and instructions well in advance of your workshop. This is good advice when giving any kind of a presentation, and Cafeteria Learning is no exception. Accordingly, to avoid surprises, you should test your activities internally and adjust them as necessary prior to rolling them out. Gather a number of your employees, colleagues, and friends and run through each of your proposed activities. You should ask or observe:

- Are the instructions clear and will learners understand how to participate in each activity?

- Are the materials working as intended?
- Are the activities producing the intended learning outcome?
- Which activities do learners really take to, and are there any that they do not like?
- Do any other problems arise that may require troubleshooting?

It is also helpful to pilot the workshop when time and resources allow, which involves testing your activities with a segment of your target population and, if possible, using the specific room in which the workshop will take place. Individuals will take to activities differently, so this will allow you to get more targeted feedback about what works best for your particular audience. Give yourself at least a week before your workshop to refine your delivery and become comfortable with all the workshop components. Plan to arrive prepared with a thorough knowledge of the content and activities. Ideally, you should know the content, how Cafeteria Learning works, and the instructions for each activity well enough to translate the experience into your own words.

## Allow for Adequate Setup Time the Day of the Workshop

Imagine the feeling of arriving to the room early with plenty of time to spare. You are calm, cool, and collected as you set up the activities. By the time the learners arrive, everything's in its place and you're ready to greet each person walking through the door. Start your workshop off on the right foot by allowing yourself plenty of time to set up the activities prior to the course start time (90 minutes, just to be safe). This way, the entire experience will be smooth, even if unexpected challenges arise.

## Prepare the Room Setup

Setting up your activities takes a bit of strategy. The best way to do it will depend on your particular space and activities. Figure 7-1 illustrates a setup blueprint. The activities are grouped by topic: for example, the activities for Topic 1 are set up on the left side of the room, the activities for Topic 2 are set up down the middle of the room, and the activities for Topic 3 are set up along the right side of the room. Note that some activities require wall space (several of the activities in Topic 1, for example);

whereas others require table space only (for example, Topic 2, Activities 1 and 2; Topic 3, Activities 1 and 2).

You might consider having your learners sit down at the central tables as you present the introductory content; throughout the rest of the workshop, the learners are free to move around the room and explore.

In addition, set up the activities that require more space, either on a wall or on tables, in each topic first, and then group the other activities for that topic around them. For example, when setting up the activities you would want to allot enough space for a collaborative activity where learners are writing or drawing on a large sheet of paper hanging on the wall. Once you find enough room for this particular activity, you can dedicate the nearby space for the other two activities in the same topic.

As you set up your activities, mark each table with an instruction sheet, including the name of the activity, the topic, and the corresponding instructions. You may also want to place a few extra copies of the instructions on the table so learners can easily grab a copy and take a look at them without having to huddle around the table.

## During the Workshop

Now it's time to greet learners at the door, welcoming them to the workshop and directing them to get started on the priming activity as they enter the room. This is an important way to set the foundation for the rest of your workshop: Without direction from a greeter, many learners will habitually head straight to their seats without even realizing that they're missing out on the priming activity.

You might also suggest that learners leave their coats, purses, and other belongings in a central location, because they won't be sitting in one place with them during the workshop. Having too many belongings at a table can create cluttered activity stations.

Once learners have settled into their seats, guide them through the final steps of your priming activity by having them answer discussion questions with a partner or share their answers with the group. This will lead you seamlessly into the rest of your workshop agenda.

Figure 7-1. Room Setup Diagram

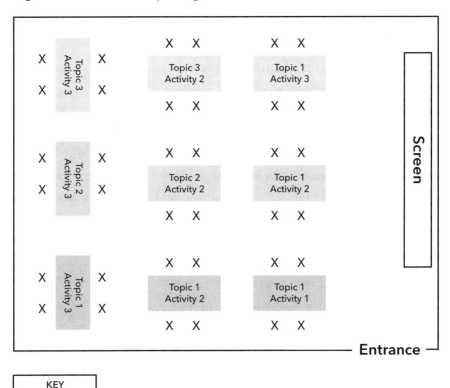

You might also include the priming questions as part of your introductory presentation, leave handouts on the tables or chairs where learners will be sitting, or both.

## Break Up Side Conversations and Keep Learners on Track

Learners are accountable for their own learning and are free to move through the activities at their own pace; however, part of your role entails helping learners stay on topic and manage their time. To help them keep tabs on time, we've found it helpful to display a countdown timer on our presentation display that they can reference throughout the workshop.

It's also a good idea to walk around the room during the workshop to find out how learners are doing and to keep them moving from one activity to another. If it's obvious that a particular learner is off track or has gotten caught up in side conversations, feel free to give her a nudge by asking something like, "Have you completed an activity in each topic yet?"

### Offer Your Learners Some Dessert

Don't leave your learners hanging: A good debriefing activity is like the cherry on top of an already delectable learning experience. When the main course, or activities, are completed, it's time to bring all the learners back together as a group to validate, for you and for them, that learning has indeed taken place. Debriefing helps bring a sense of completion to your workshop and allows your learners to leave your workshop feeling satisfied and full.

## After the Workshop

Before you break down your activities, take a moment to snap a few pictures of your learners' creations. Not only will this give you a chance to admire the fruits of your labor, it will also help to remind you what worked and what could be improved next time.

The best learning experiences aren't singular, one-time events; rather, they're spread out over time and are reinforced in a variety of ways. About 30 days after the workshop, send out follow-up communications (emails, notecards) to those who participated in the workshop. In your communications include:

- a brief paragraph or two to refresh their memories on key takeaways from the workshop
- attachments or links to photos showing output from the workshop to remind them of the work they did
- a question or two about how they've incorporated the knowledge or skills into their day-to-day work, and a friendly nudge to take action if they haven't yet done so.

## Summary

Cafeteria Learning relies on facilitation, not presentation. As a facilitator your role is to be a guide during the experience, helping learners to learn from the provided content, one another, and their experiences. Differing from a more traditional training presentation, during which you are the expert in the room, your job is to ensure that learners:

- Understand the Cafeteria Learning concept.
- Successfully complete their chosen activities.
- Stay engaged and on track.

# 8

# MEASURING AND EVALUATING THE RESULTS

When you make your workshop available, how do you know it will be successful? This is a concern for the learning professional and for those sponsoring the learning initiative. When measuring success you need to ask, "Did the learners' behavior change as a result of participating in the learning experience?"

## Create a Measurement Plan

Creating a plan to gather measurement metrics is integral to any learning experience, and evaluating the results of a Cafeteria Learning workshop is not all that different from evaluating other learning methods. Planning allows you to identify the data to collect so you can validate that the learning outcome has been achieved. With Cafeteria Learning, you can start your measurement plan by asking questions such as:

- Were the learning objectives met?
- Did learners enjoy the learning experience?
- Did they learn something?
- Are they applying what they learned?
- What impact did their learning have on the organization?
- Were there unintentional outcomes of the learning experience for the organization?

Without a measurement plan, you'll miss out on the opportunity to understand whether your workshop achieved the desired results, so it's critically important to think about what you want to measure in the early stages of creating a learning experience. When considering your measurement metrics, the best place to start is usually by examining both your desired learning outcome and your stated learning objectives.

For a Cafeteria Learning workshop, the measurement plan can be simple: Using the learning objectives, you can survey the learners before and after the workshop to evaluate, on a scale of 1-5 with 5 being highest, the effectiveness of the learning. On the day of the workshop, before getting started, you or the facilitator can ask each learner to complete a quick survey with questions aligned to the learning objectives and again, at the end of the workshop. For a workshop on training your sales team, you might ask, "Are you able to identify the basic components of the sales process?"

## Unintended Outcomes

Sometimes, no matter how much you plan, the learning may result in unintended outcomes. In other words, there may be outcomes not directly related to the intended outcomes or objectives, but that may nevertheless arise as a result of the learning initiative. We have yet to find a formula to officially plan and prepare for these occurrences, but we found if we are open to them, they may just present themselves.

One good example of an unintended outcome in Cafeteria Learning is that learners will often form new business relationships with co-workers due to the social and interactive nature of the methodology. Although this may not be one of the primary objectives or intended outcomes, it is a beneficial side effect that's worth measuring. Our measurement metric in this case might be the number of learners who formed new business relationships with colleagues. Some other unintended outcomes as a result of a Cafeteria Learning experience may be:

- Learners are highly engaged, contributing to an increased ability to retain content.

- Learning is experiential, which has a higher translation to action and application.
- Learners experience a high degree of interaction and exchange of ideas, which clearly honors others' perspectives and adds depth and perspective to their own.
- Learners learn through opportunities to teach and share with others.
- Learners practice their active listening skills.
- Learners are able to characterize what they have gained from the learning experience, even without explicitly stating the course objectives.

## Implementing a Measurement Plan

Now that you have an idea of what you want to measure, consider how you want to measure your stated metrics. For example, how might you evaluate your learners' ability to explain three strategies to implement brain-based learning principles? There is no one way to measure a metric; numerous methods exist for capturing and evaluating data. For this example, let's use the Kirkpatrick Partners method of evaluation, which is based on four levels of evaluation.

## Level 1 Reaction

Measure immediately at the end of the workshop. How did learners react to the learning immediately after completing it? Level 1 is the most basic of the four levels, and it doesn't on its own help you evaluate whether the learning objectives or intended outcome were met. When used in combination with other levels of measurement, it can be a useful tool for gauging participants' levels of engagement and enjoyment, which is valuable in its own right. Some common methods for Level 1 include:

- asking learners questions about their reactions to the learning experience
- asking learners to complete comment cards
- observing engagement levels during the workshop
- receiving spontaneous feedback.

## Level 2 Learning

Measure before, during, or immediately at the end of the workshop. How much did the learners learn? Level 2 evaluates the skills or knowledge that learners have acquired as a result of the learning. In other words, have the learning objectives been met? Some common methods for Level 2 include:

- immediately evaluating the knowledge the learners have at the end of the workshop
- implementing a pre-test/post-test to determine how skills and knowledge have increased as a result of the learning
- asking participants what they've learned and documenting their feedback.

## Level 3 Behavior

Measure 30 to 90 days after the end of the workshop. How have learners changed their behavior? Level 3 seeks to determine whether learners are actually applying what they've learned in their day-to-day work at least 30 days after the workshop. You will want to make sure to provide enough time for learners to synthesize and apply the learning. Some common methods for Level 3 include:

- surveying the manager of an employee to assess whether the employee's behavior has changed
- asking learners to describe how or if they are applying the learning
- observing learners in their day-to-day working environment.

## Level 4 Results

Measure at least 90 days after the end of the workshop. What are the results to the organization? Is there a change in the business as a result of learners applying what they've learned? Has the desired business outcome been achieved? When learners are provided with tools to apply what they learned and using them results in a clear business impact, a correlation between learning and results can be made. Methods for evaluating Level 4 results will differ depending on the intended business outcomes, but often come in the form of hard metrics such as:

- monitoring key performance indicators, such as sales volume or generation of new business (when the targeted outcome is increased sales volume)
- capturing employee turnover rates (when the targeted outcome is decreased turnover)
- asking customers their level of satisfaction (when the targeted outcome is increased customer satisfaction rates).

With Level 4 evaluation being the most challenging to measure but worth the effort, consider these broad guidelines: Establish reliable points of reference, allow enough time for change to occur, and continue to measure results at specific points after the workshop. And remember that Level 4 might not be appropriate for all learning efforts; a cost-benefit analysis can help save you from wasted resources when a simpler level of evaluation may have been more appropriate.

## Using Baseline Metrics

Another important piece of the measurement and evaluation process involves capturing baseline metrics. After all, the relevance of the data captured during this process can only become clear when compared with a baseline metric. For example, capturing a business unit's sales volume tells you little unless you can compare it with sales volume in the periods preceding your sales training. Did sales volume increase or decrease from the baseline metric?

When establishing baseline metrics, consider sources of existing data and pre-program questions you might want to ask. Look at the organization or business unit that you are creating the learning experience for and identify existing data they are already capturing. You might be able to use these data as a baseline metric for a measurement plan.

If you were to design a Cafeteria Learning workshop for performance reviews, for example, you could consult with HR to identify the information they are already tracking. With the outcome being to increase managers' ability to set clear expectations for employees and hold them accountable for results, data around the number of performance improvement plans could be captured. Because HR has years of data on this metric, it can become one of the baseline metrics to help evaluate whether the desired outcome was being met as a result of the learning. An increase in performance improvement plans would be evidence that the managers were applying the skills they developed around setting clear expectations and holding employees accountable.

## Summary

Measuring and evaluating may provide proof that the desired learning outcome and objectives were met, the learning experience investment was worthwhile, and the learning effort had a positive impact on the business. Careful evaluation can ultimately help you demonstrate the value that progressive learning models such as Cafeteria Learning can hold for your organization.

# 9

# CASE STUDIES

We first introduced the concept of Cafeteria Learning to learners at the ASTD Cascadia Chapter's 2012 conference "Back to Basics and Beyond." Since that time, we have refined the method to its current form. This chapter presents some of our case studies with reactions from learners and organizations who were keen to participate in this new method of learning.

## ASTD Cascadia Chapter 2012 Conference: "The Brain Is Not a Bucket" Session

*Note: This was the first use of the Cafeteria Learning method; the process has been refined quite a bit since this workshop. For example, we learned from this experience that while five activities per topic provides ample choice for learners, it is a large undertaking for a learning designer and also requires a lot of complex preparation for facilitators.*

The brain is not a finite container that you fill up. Instead, the brain is a complex system of dynamic connections that interpret, process, and organize an amazing amount of information. Most of our learning takes place through direct experience as opposed to formal instruction.

This workshop presented at the ASTD Cascadia Chapter's 2012 conference "Back to Basics and Beyond" looked at the shortcomings of traditional lecture-based learning and education through the filter of brain-based learning research. What roles do experience and sensory intake play in learning? How can we implement brain-based learning principles to get back to the basics and create richer, longer-lasting learning experiences?

The hands-on workshop, facilitated by Idea Learning Group, was designed to help learners reframe the way they train using practical brain-based tools and strategies with their learners. The room was organized into three learning topics, each with five separate activity stations. Here are three activities from the workshop:

## Engaging Your Audience (Topic: Best Practices)

(individual or pair; reflective; low tech)

Flipcharts were prepared ahead of time with the following titles, "Instead of Butts in Seats, Try . . . ," "Instead of Pre-Determining Outcomes, Try . . . ," "Instead of Lectures, Try . . . ," and "Instead of Slides, Try . . . ." When learners arrived at the station, they were asked to think about or discuss alternatives to traditional learning approaches. For each situation listed on the flipcharts, learners wrote lists such as:

- Going outside.
- Role plays or simulations.
- Allowing learners to construct their own outcomes.
- Asking learners to discover content.
- Scavenger hunts.
- Teach back activities.

## Brainly Land (Topic: Brain-Based Learning)

(group; collaboration or competition; low tech)

A group of up to four players participates in a game that quizzes their knowledge of brain-based learning. In turn, players roll dice and advance the appropriate number of spaces. If a player lands on a BRAIN square, choose a BRAIN card from the deck. Read the card out loud to the group, and keep it until the game ends. The first one who reaches the end is not necessarily the winner! Accumulated knowledge—brain cards—counts for something, too:

- The first person to reach the end is awarded 5 points.
- The second person to reach the end is awarded 4 points.
- The third person to reach the end is awarded 3 points.
- The players are also awarded 1 point per brain card they have.

## Limber Learning (Topic: Limitations of Lectures)

(individual; kinesthetic; low tech)

Staying glued to your seat during lectures is not only boring, but also unhealthy. New research shows that it's best to stand up and move around for two minutes out of every 20 minutes during the day. It helps keep you energized, focused, and healthy. Learners try five yoga-inspired exercises they can apply in their learning sessions. For example, Exercise 1: Breathe With Intention! Deep breathing is essential for relaxation, clear thinking, and well-being. Try this simple exercise to maximize your breathing:

- Sit in a comfortable upright position, on a chair or on the floor.
- Inhale through your nose and count to four.
- Briefly hold the breath in and count to two.
- Exhale through your nose and count to four.
- Count to four before beginning the cycle again.
- Repeat 10 times.

## Approaching Brain Science Differently

The "Back to Basics and Beyond" conference asked the 46 participants at the end of all sessions to evaluate their experience by answering three questions. Table 9-1 presents the results.

Table 9-1. Reactions to First Cafeteria Learning Workshop

| | Strongly Agree | Agree | Neutral | Disagree | Strongly Disagree |
|---|---|---|---|---|---|
| The Speaker Was Effective | 57% | 37% | 6% | 0% | 0% |
| The Topic Was Relevant to Me and the Work I Do | 73% | 22% | 5% | 0% | 0% |

Table 9-1. Reactions to First Cafeteria Learning Workshop (cont.)

| | Strongly Agree | Agree | Neutral | Disagree | Strongly Disagree |
|---|---|---|---|---|---|
| This Session Provided Good Value for My Time | 49% | 40% | 7% | 2% | 2% |

# The Virginia Garcia Memorial Health Center

In December 2015, the diversity and inclusion ready-to-go kit Diversity Works was piloted with a group of 18 staff members at the Oregon-based Virginia Garcia Memorial Health Center. Diversity Works is an off-the-shelf solution designed to help organizations implement a Cafeteria Learning workshop with a complete set of materials and instructions on the subject of diversity and inclusion.

"The style of learning was different than the traditional way," a learner stated. "But I liked that it gave me the flexibility to participate in the activities I'm more comfortable with. You pick what you want to do, you pick what you want to achieve."

The Virginia Garcia Clinic was formed in 1975, when 6-year-old Virginia Garcia, the daughter of migrant farm workers, tragically passed away as a result of complications from a cut on her foot—a wound that should have been easily treatable were it not for the language, cultural, and economic barriers standing in the way of receiving proper medical care. The founders of Virginia Garcia vowed to prevent anything like this from happening again, and a mission was born. Ever since, the nonprofit has been providing culturally appropriate healthcare to migrant workers and other individuals who face barriers in receiving medical care.

To provide choice for learners, we set up the materials as nine stations around the room, each of which corresponded to one of the workshop's three main learning objectives: Identify what makes me the unique individual I am, seek to understand others, and consider differing perspectives in the workplace. Here are three activities from the workshop:

## Uniquely Me (Topic: Understanding Self)

(individual; reflective; low tech)

Several sheets of paper were placed on a table along with sticker shapes of various colors. Learners used the sticker shapes to craft a representation of themselves on paper then finish the sentence: "I am unique because . . ." Learners were instructed to hang their creations on the wall for others to see.

## Telling My Story (Topic: Understanding Others)

(individual; reflective; high tech)

A recording device was placed on a table along with several story prompts, such as: "Describe a time when you experienced another person's bias," "Tell about a time as a child that you observed an adult who was disrespectful toward someone," and "Tell about a time when you stood up for someone else." Learners selected a story prompt then recorded their answer. Learners also had the option to review stories recorded by others and answer the question, "What stood out to you as you viewed others' stories?" on a flipchart.

## Communicate With Care (Topic: Communication)

(individual, partner, or group; reflective; low tech)

Learners spun a wheel to land on a scenario related to communication in the workplace and then shared their answers to the two discussion questions on a "perspective card." Cards were left at the station for others to review.

At the end of the workshop, the learners all came together for a final shared experience and participated in a diversity and inclusion board game.

## Journey of Diversity

(group; collaborative; low tech)

Learners were organized into small groups of five. Each group received a board game, card set, dice, and game pieces. Learners participated in the game by individually answering questions related to diversity and inclusion and advancing spaces on the board with each correct answer.

## Coming Together Through Diversity

Shared experience turned out to be an unintended outcome for the learning and provided insight among learners. Learning through shared experiences is constructivism in action: Learners construct and discover meaning and knowledge through active exploration rather than having it presented to them in a lecture. For many of the activities, there were no right or wrong answers; rather, the bulk of the learning occurred through the learners' impressions, thoughts, and perspectives as they moved through various activities and interacted with their peers. One activity, for example, had learners identify their initial reaction to a specific diversity and inclusion scenario. They then took the time to think through a more appropriate response.

"When [my group] shared our responses with each other, I was surprised that all three of us had the same reaction initially, but then we all decided to respond thoughtfully in a slightly different way," shared one learner. "It's both showing diversity and the fact that in a ton of ways we're the same. It was interesting that the learning was driven by what we were saying to each other in the moment rather than from what we're hearing in a rote presentation."

"Those 'aha moments' will stick with me," he continued. "I will remember that [my group] came together, we disagreed, then at the end we were able to kind of look back and reflect and say, 'Oh yeah, you know what, there is a different way to look at this, maybe there is a different feeling to those words or to how we approach a situation.' That's what I took from it, and I don't see myself forgetting that, especially since I did it and I didn't just sit and listen."

"This experience made me think in so many ways," another learner shared. "At the same time I learned how other people think."

Yet another learner contrasted the workshop to a lecture the team had attended in the very same room the day before. "Yesterday we were in this same space [for a learning experience], sitting in chairs all day long," she explained. "It was frustrating because I think that people learn better when they're up and moving their bodies. Moving around is definitely my chosen way to learn; I think it engages people more when you do that, and I liked that there were three different options for each category so if we weren't comfortable doing one activity, then maybe we'd be comfortable doing another one. For example, I didn't choose to record a history of myself. That was not one that I'd want to do. I did the drawing station instead; I'm not an artist, but it was fun."

In a post-workshop survey, more than a third of learners indicated that they had shared personal experiences related to the topic with others. The results of the post-workshop survey reinforced the idea that learning in an active, choice-based way is an effective way to learn. In our evaluation, learners indicated that they are most likely to definitely learn by participating in activities (68 percent), followed by being given a choice of how to learn (65 percent), sharing their own knowledge (53 percent), and lastly, through lecture (50 percent).

"I would love to see my continuing medical education credits offered in this manner," shared a Virginia Garcia staff member, "because those of us who go to these lectures all day long are bored to death and we know that we don't get much out of it. I like this format and I think it should be incorporated more into what we do here as adults—and also at school where our children are learning."

Eric Oslund, employee performance and talent development manager, said, "What's really great about this is that I can run it. I need a handful of people, but I don't need outside expertise to run this workshop. Anybody can run this stuff, which is great."

## Wellness at Kimpton Hotels & Restaurants

With a business goal to build a culture at Kimpton Hotels & Restaurants that encourages healthy behaviors that influence and inspire others to achieve a balance of wellness, and just two hours available for learning time, the company found that the Cafeteria Learning method was an effective choice for this custom content. The rollout of this wellness program involved a train-the-trainer model, so the experience could be implemented across 35 locations nationwide as quickly and efficiently as possible. Here are three activities from the workshop:

## Strength or Challenge
## (Topic 1: The Kimpton Wellness Wheel)

(partner; reflective or problem solving; low tech)

Learners took turns spinning a "Wellness Wheel," which was displayed at the center of the table, and sharing their answers to the following questions: "Is the area of the Wellness Wheel you landed on a strength or a challenge for you?" "If this area is a strength, what best practices can you share?" and "If it's a challenge, what is getting in your way?"

## Take Your Temperature (Topic 2: My Wellness WIG)

(individual; reflective or visual; low tech)

At Kimpton, a wellness WIG is a wildly important goal related to one or more elements of wellness on their Wellness Wheel. Images of six thermometers were hung on the wall, with five pairs of green and black dry-erase markers placed on a table. Learners took turns rating their current state of wellness for each area of well-being by making marks on each thermometer using the black marker ("taking their temperature").

Next, learners used the green markers to rate where they would like their wellness to be for each area of well-being, writing their name next to each mark. Lastly, learners reflected on two questions: "Are your temperatures where you want them to be?" and "Which area(s) would you like to see change?"

This activity was a great way to help learners assess and reflect on their current and desired levels of wellness to help inform their wildly important goal.

## My Wellness WIG (Topic 2: My Wellness WIG)

(individual; reflective; low tech)

In this activity, learners wore novelty headband "wigs" to get their creative juices flowing as they brainstormed personal wellness WIGs related to a specific area of well-being (physical, career, financial, community, social, or internal balance).

To jog their memory on the definition of WIGs, we first asked learners to think back to the workshop's foundational content in which they learned about WIGs and refer to some examples of WIGs that we displayed at the station for their reference. Learners then drafted a wellness WIG in their personal wellness workbooks; if they felt comfortable sharing their WIG, they could also write it on one of the flipcharts displayed on the wall (the "Wellness WIG Gallery").

## Taking Time for Wellness

For employees who often feel stressed and pressed for time, it was a true gift to be able to slow down and think about how to foster a sense of well-being in their lives. Learners also enjoyed the social and interactive nature of the Cafeteria Learning workshop. "I liked interacting with the other people in the room and bouncing ideas off each other and realizing that we were all in the same boat," said one learner after the workshop.

"Being allowed the time, at work, to think about my own personal wellness was like an emotional massage!" said another.

Learners left the workshop with personally crafted wellness goals, along with corresponding action plans to achieve them. Kimpton management is thrilled with the results and excited to continue offering the wellness workshop to new and seasoned employees each year.

# Daimler Trucks North America (DTNA)

On a Wednesday afternoon in Portland, Oregon, sunlight streamed into a glass-paneled conference room at the corporate headquarters of Daimler Trucks, the largest heavy-duty truck manufacturer in North America. A group of employees was gathered together to participate in a pilot study of the Cafeteria Learning ready-to-go kit, Diversity Works. (This is the same kit that was used for the Cafeteria Learning pilot with Virginia Garcia; thus, similar activities were utilized.) The Diversity Works product consists of an array of nine predesigned diversity and inclusion activities that a facilitator can set up and implement with minimal time and effort. Daimler Trucks employees came together to participate in the pilot study from several departments, including finance, IT, HR, diversity, and legal.

We began by facilitating an initial priming activity and presenting learners with a brief introduction, and then we set them free to explore and tinker around the room. Throughout the workshop, learners enjoyed the opportunity to take control of and choose their own learning, to interact and engage with other learners, and to learn experientially.

"When you go to a lot of workshops, there's a lot of lecture and then they might have you do an activity that feels forced, but nobody wants to get up at that point because they've already settled into their seats," one learner said. "This was nice in that while there was a brief introduction, you were moving around the entire time and not getting too comfortable. I think that helps you to be engaged in each topic and to really learn."

"I do like the idea of the cafeteria," added another learner. "It provides different options, it keeps you moving, and it allows you to go through and look at the same concept in different ways. I like learning through engagement and being involved, but most trainings don't offer much engagement at all, and those that do only engage you in one way. They don't give you the choices where you can move from activity to activity and have different ways of learning like Cafeteria Learning does."

Learners also noted that they felt empowered by the inherent choice that the approach offers. "I thought it was a very unique way to approach training," shared one learner. "I think by giving folks the ability to choose what they learn or the style in which they want to learn, you open them up to learn more, because they're selecting the activities and they feel empowered. So I think it's a very powerful opportunity to take ownership of your learning."

He noted that he chose certain types of activities over others and appreciated having a variety of activities to choose from: "I chose not to go to the drawing station because that makes me very uncomfortable, so I liked the idea of being able to mix it up a little bit."

Another employee took the opposite approach, consciously choosing activities that pushed him outside his comfort zone: "I made a conscious choice to pick an activity that made me feel uncomfortable because I knew that if I got in my comfort zone, I may not be able to learn more, whereas if I made myself a little bit uncomfortable maybe I could make myself vulnerable, which opens me up to learn."

"[My partner and I] both wanted to do the same stuff," another man added, "and I found out why—we started talking, and it turns out he does the same kind of work that I do and we have the same mindset on how work gets done. I realized that he picked the same kind of analytical stuff as I did—solving the puzzle, the case studies, and [problem solving] because I can't draw."

Experiences like this not only speak to the idea of allowing for individuals' unique learning preferences, but also illustrate how the social and interactive nature of Cafeteria Learning opens up opportunities for learners to form new relationships with their peers—or to deepen those that may already exist.

"I'm from Eastern Europe," one woman said, extending her hand as she introduced herself to a man she'd partnered with for an activity. "I'm from Virginia," the man responded. The two of them delved into the activity together; within minutes, they were deep in discussion.

At another table, two women shared with each other about the diverse qualities that make them the unique individuals they are, touching on topics such as spirituality ("I believe in a higher calling"), hobbies ("You won't believe how much I love bowling!"), and personal challenges ("I'm dyslexic"). In a post-workshop survey, 80 percent of learners indicated that they had shared personal experiences related to the topic with others. More than half of learners indicated that others shared personal experiences with them that they were able to learn from as well.

In addition to sharing about themselves, learners also exchanged their thoughts and viewpoints on various topics. While playing a diversity and inclusion board game, employees clapped when their peers answered a question right, occasionally pausing to discuss one of the questions among themselves. "Is that really the definition of homophobia?" one man asked.

For the next few minutes, the group ping-ponged their thoughts back and forth among one another.

"This workshop was valuable because it actually allowed people to exchange viewpoints," commented one learner.

This kind of shared discussion and interaction is a key driver for experiential learning. One activity, for example, was aimed at helping learners understand the concept of unconscious bias. At a typical training session, a lecturer might present the definition of unconscious bias and explain to learners why it's important to be aware of and to challenge the biases they form in their interactions with others.

In Cafeteria Learning, however, the learning happens more directly. By choosing a photo of a stranger and answering discussion questions about the person they chose, learners began to gain an understanding of their own unconscious biases. Based on a single snapshot of a person and a few facts about his occupation and hometown, learners began to realize that they had already formed snap judgments about whether they liked and trusted that person, about the person's lifestyle and beliefs, and so on.

"He looks important and too serious," one woman shared in reference to the photo of a man she had picked. "I don't trust him."

Another woman guessed that the woman in her photo, who was employed as a nanny, had a high-school education.

"We all automatically form judgments and biases as we interact with the people around us," the facilitator explained as she guided the group in their learning experience. "It's the way our brains work, and it's neither good nor bad. It only becomes a problem when we are unaware of these judgments and carry them into our relationships without questioning their accuracy or validity. The point is to become aware of our unconscious biases and know that we have them so that we can learn to challenge them and not to carry them unexamined into our relationships with others."

Several learners nodded their heads in agreement as the facilitator spoke. They weren't just being lectured about an abstract concept; rather, they were experiencing their own unconscious bias in a concrete way.

"I wanted it to be provocative, and it was," said Daimler Trucks Learning and Development Manager Brian Stowe.

And learners appeared to have an appetite for more: In a post-workshop survey, 87 percent of learners indicated that they'd enjoy learning about another topic through Cafeteria Learning.

# PeaceHealth

At PeaceHealth, a not-for-profit health system serving communities in Washington, Oregon, and Alaska, Erica Davis acknowledges diversity in how adults learn by applying the Cafeteria Learning model to an annual two-day conference on population health. Davis, a learning and leadership development program manager for PeaceHealth, immediately identified with the Cafeteria Learning technique when she learned about it at her local ATD chapter conference; she recognized the importance of staying up-to-date with what is "up and coming" in the learning and development field.

As the learning designer for one 60-minute session at the conference with a cohort of 80 clinical leaders attending, Davis determined a Cafeteria Learning experience would allow for more content sharing than a more traditional presentation. The method would allow participants to choose activities that appealed to them. It was a risk, with most of the audience accustomed to typical lecture-style learning, but with the support of the stakeholder, she was ready to give it a try.

With objectives in mind, Davis utilized existing activities and pulled from her experience as a learner to build activities at four stations. Each station included a variety of activities that achieved the same outcome, regardless of what the learner completed. An activity worksheet listing the activities was used by participants as a guide when selecting activities to participate in.

Activity stations were set up in various locations around the conference location to accommodate the large audience. Since this experience was her first time implementing Cafeteria Learning, Davis acted as a floating facilitator to answer any questions while she relied on facilitators at each station to ensure participation. A week before the session, Davis held a meeting with each facilitator explaining how the model works, the learning concepts, and people's roles at their assigned station. Having an experienced facilitator at each station aided in gathering data and ensuring that the activities were executed properly.

Learners watched video clips illustrating the social determinants of health and brainstormed in small groups how they could create solutions for similar patients in their local communities. Others participated in mind-mapping scenarios to develop community safety nets through leveraging social services and community partners for vulnerable patient populations. A game involved learners in practicing the steps of leading improvement projects and illustrated the impact of communication. Other activities included case studies and discussions.

## Social Determinants of Health Video Clips

(group; collaborative; high tech)

A screen was set up to play video clips that illustrated social effects of individuals' health. In small groups, learners were asked to brainstorm ways they could create solutions for similar patients in their local communities. The conversation was monitored by a facilitator stationed at the activity and the information was gathered using flipcharts.

## Community Safety Nets Mind Mapping

(individual, partner, or group; reflective; low tech)

Individuals or groups of two or more were given a scenario that dealt with safety nets in the communities represented by various PeaceHealth medical centers, particularly within their vulnerable patient populations. The learners were asked to mind map solutions and outcomes leveraging the social services and community partners available to patients.

## Impact of Communication Board Game

(group; collaborative; low tech)

Learners were organized into small groups and used a board game that included trivia cards, dice, and game pieces. As part of the game, they answered questions, practiced the steps of leading improvement projects, and discussed the impact of communication.

## Breaking Out of Accustomed Models

The feedback from this session was highly positive overall. The session was "just as good if not better than if we would have done instructor-led training," said one participant. All of the participants agreed or strongly agreed that this activity met the learning objectives for being able to describe leadership behaviors for improving the health of vulnerable populations.

Participants shared the following feedback: "I enjoyed the activities and working with people I have never met before." "I learn best by being involved and being hands on." "[Facilitators] kept us engaged through activities and getting up and moving around." "Activities around different topics were very helpful in understanding different concepts."

Some learners did mention they were uncomfortable with the session format and preferred lecture-style learning. Some facilitators also stated they preferred to be at the front of the room leading the learning, rather than relying on the learners to discover the information. Unlike many of her instructor-led sessions, Davis noted that this method gave her the opportunity to hear feedback from participants immediately, in the moment, and it stretched both participants and facilitators to engage in learning in a new way. Looking back, Davis recommends that other learning designers using Cafeteria Learning ensure that the debrief process happens. This was one component that she'll be sure to spend more time designing and implementing next time.

# 10

# TRIED-AND-TRUE CAFETERIA LEARNING ACTIVITIES

Mix and match this handpicked selection of our most popular and versatile activities to use as starting points for your Cafeteria Learning design process. Use them for your own activity menu, or use them as a springboard for coming up with new or modified activities. Feel free to change the structure and the materials of each activity to meet your needs.

Most of these activities can be applied to a variety of topics, but sometimes an activity may work best within one particular subject matter context. The "Happy Hopper" activity is an example of an activity that we use specifically for communication—in this case, for teaching managers to give their employees specific (rather than general) praise: for example, "I love how much detail you included in your presentation" rather than "Great job!"

As you review this selection, you'll notice we used the design document as your guide. The Topic Title, Learning Objectives, Foundational Content, Activity Title, and Reflection Questions sections are purposefully left out so you can tailor the activity to meet your content and learning needs.

| Topic Title (Priming) | Learning Objective | | |
|---|---|---|---|

**Foundational Content**

| Activity Title (Priming) | | | Estimated Time 10 minutes |
|---|---|---|---|

**Activity Description**

Participants choose randomly from a set of cards with thought-provoking quotes. They then answer discussion questions about the card they chose.

| Learning Preference | | Interaction | Technology |
|---|---|---|---|
| ☐ Problem solving<br>☐ Competition | ☐ Collaboration<br>☒ Visual | ☐ Auditory<br>☐ Kinesthetic | ☒ Reflective | ☒ Individual<br>☒ Partner | ☐ Group<br>☐ Other | ☐ High tech<br>☒ Low tech |

**Activity Instructions**

Priming activities are facilitated; therefore, you will not need to print out instruction sheets for this activity. Our instructions for the facilitator's use are as follows:

1. When participants enter the room, instruct them to take one quote card.
2. After the session begins, ask participants to read their quote card and then share it with people at their table.

**Reflection Questions**

Ask if anyone would like to share his or her quote with the group.

Ask what learners noticed about the themes of their quotes.

| Produce | Purchase | Workshop Materials |
|---|---|---|
| | | Large poster board with hook-and-loop pieces. You'll attach each quote card to this board for participants to choose from as they enter the room. |
| | | Laminated quote cards displaying a variety of images or thought-provoking quotes, one for each participant, plus a few extra for choice. Each card has a hook-and-loop piece stuck to the back of it for easy attachment to the poster board. |
| | | Printed copies of the discussion questions, one for each participant. |

**Topic Title**

**Learning Objective**

**Foundational Content**

**Activity Title**
(Case Studies)

**Estimated Time**
10 minutes

**Activity Description**
Participants choose a case study (from a set of three) to work on and answer questions at the end of each case study. Case studies are a great way to flex your learners' problem-solving muscles and to get them actively thinking and talking about how they can apply the concepts to real-life situations.

**Learning Preference**

☒ Problem solving
☐ Competition
☐ Collaboration
☐ Visual
☐ Auditory
☐ Kinesthetic
☐ Reflective

**Interaction**

☐ Individual
☒ Partner
☒ Group
☐ Other

**Technology**

☐ High tech
☒ Low tech

**Activity Instructions**
1. Choose one of the case studies.
2. Read the case study aloud and answer the questions with a partner or group.

**Reflection Questions**

| Produce | Purchase | Workshop Materials |
|---|---|---|
| | | Laminated activity instructions. |
| | | Table and chairs. |
| | | One copy of each case study and questions. (We usually like to create about three case studies, each printed on a separate sheet of paper.) |

| Topic Title | Learning Objective |
|---|---|

**Foundational Content**

| Activity Title | | Estimated Time |
|---|---|---|
| (Conversation Cards) | | 10 minutes |

**Activity Description**

With a partner, participants take turns choosing cards and discussing the respective questions on each card. Conversation cards contain content meant to be thought-provoking. This type of activity is an excellent way to allow participants to state their own thoughts and opinions while also learning from someone else's thoughts.

**Learning Preference**

☒ Problem solving
☐ Competition
☐ Collaboration
☐ Visual
☐ Auditory
☐ Kinesthetic
☒ Reflective

**Interaction**

☐ Individual
☒ Partner
☐ Group
☐ Other

**Technology**

☐ High tech
☒ Low tech

**Activity Instructions**

1. Choose a conversation card.
2. Read the card aloud and discuss with your partner.
3. Switch roles until all the cards have been read and discussed.

**Reflection Questions**

| Produce | Purchase | Workshop Materials |
|---|---|---|
| | | Laminated activity instructions. |
| | | Table and chairs. |
| | | 18 conversation questions printed on 5x7 cards, laminated. |

**Topic Title**

**Learning Objective**

**Foundational Content**

**Activity Title**
(Happy Hopper)

**Estimated Time**
10 minutes

**Activity Description**
Standing in a circle, learners take turns giving examples based on a hypothetical situation. Each time a learner contributes her example, she winds the "happy hopper" windup toy one time before passing it on to the next learner in the circle. After everyone has had a turn, the last learner lets the happy hopper go on the table.

**Learning Preference**

☒ Collaboration ☐ Auditory ☐ Reflective
☐ Problem solving ☐ Visual ☐ Kinesthetic
☐ Competition

**Interaction**

☐ Individual ☒ Group
☐ Partner ☐ Other

**Technology**

☐ High tech
☒ Low tech

**Activity Instructions**
1. Stand in a circle, facing one another. Read the scenario. Think of a single, specific example.
2. Say your example aloud, wind the happy hopper, and while holding the feet, pass it to the next person.
3. Continue until everyone has had a turn to say their examples. Examples cannot be duplicated.
4. Set the happy hopper down on the table and watch it go!

**Reflection Questions**

| Produce | Purchase | Workshop Materials |
|---|---|---|
| | | Laminated activity instructions. |
| | | Table and chairs. |
| | | Windup toys (we used smiley face ones). |
| | | Employee behavior scenario cards. |

| Topic Title | Learning Objective |
| --- | --- |

**Foundational Content**

| **Activity Title** (Heads-Up!) | | **Estimated Time** 10 minutes |
| --- | --- | --- |

**Activity Description**

In pairs, learners select notecards with a word or phrase and hold them by their forehead. While their partner offers clues, learners try to guess the word or phrase. Partners take turns guessing and helping.

**Learning Preference**

| ☐ Problem solving | ☐ Collaboration | ☐ Auditory | ☐ Reflective |
| --- | --- | --- | --- |
| ☒ Competition | ☒ Visual | ☐ Kinesthetic | |

**Interaction**

☐ Individual  ☒ Partner  ☐ Group  ☐ Other

**Technology**

☒ High tech  ☐ Low tech

**Activity Instructions**

1. Determine who will be Learner 1 and who will be Learner 2.
2. Learner 1 will select notecards from the Set 1 deck, *without reading the word/phrase.*
3. One at a time, Learner 1 will place one notecard to his forehead with the word/phrase side visible for Learner 2.
4. Learner 2 will give clues to Learner 1 (without saying the word/phrase) while Learner 1 guesses what the word/phrase is.
   - Got it right? Place the notecard in the "correct" pile.
   - Got it wrong or want to skip? Place the notecard in the "discard" pile.
5. When all the notecards in Set 1 are used, learners switch roles and use Set 2 of the notecards.

**Reflection Questions**

| Produce | Purchase | Workshop Materials |
| --- | --- | --- |
| | | Laminated activity instructions. |
| | | Table and chairs. |
| | | Two sets of 20 notecards with words/phrases. |

| Topic Title | | Learning Objective | |
|---|---|---|---|

**Foundational Content**

| Activity Title | | | | Estimated Time |
|---|---|---|---|---|
| (Magnetic Poetry) | | | | 10 minutes |

**Activity Description**

Learners place words on a magnetic board to build creative phrases that relate to the selected topic.

| Learning Preference | | | Interaction | | Technology |
|---|---|---|---|---|---|
| ☐ Problem solving | ☒ Collaboration | ☐ Auditory | ☐ Reflective | ☒ Individual | ☐ Group | ☐ High tech |
| ☐ Competition | ☒ Visual | ☒ Kinesthetic | | ☐ Partner | ☐ Other | ☒ Low tech |

**Activity Instructions**

1. Place words on the board to build a creative phrase related to what comes to mind when you think of the topic.
2. You can build off phrases or sentences already on the board or create your own.

**Reflection Questions**

| Produce | Purchase | Workshop Materials |
|---|---|---|
| | | Laminated activity instructions. |
| | | Table. |
| | | One magnetic board for learners to create and display their magnetic poetry. |
| | | An easel or wall to display the magnetic poetry board. |
| | | A selection of small rectangular magnetic pieces, each with a word printed on the front. When choosing your words for this activity, come up with 25-35 sentences that you think your learners might typically create and print each of these words (even if they are duplicates). Also print at least two of each "connector" word (the, as, a, in, at, for, I, you, me, and, we, they). |

109

| Topic Title | Learning Objective |
| --- | --- |

**Foundational Content**

| **Activity Title**<br>(Mind Maps) | | **Estimated Time**<br>10 minutes |
| --- | --- | --- |

**Activity Description**

Several flipchart pages are taped together on a wall to create one large writing space. The question "What does (topic) mean to you?" is written in the center of the paper writing space. Learners add lines off the center question or off one another's responses to answer the question if they have the same response.

**Learning Preference**

| ☐ Problem solving | ☐ Collaboration | ☐ Auditory | ☒ Reflective |
| --- | --- | --- | --- |
| ☐ Competition | ☒ Visual | ☐ Kinesthetic | |

**Interaction**

| ☒ Individual | ☐ Group |
| --- | --- |
| ☐ Partner | ☐ Other |

**Technology**

| ☐ High tech |
| --- |
| ☒ Low tech |

**Activity Instructions**

1. Use markers to add lines to the mind map describing what (topic) means to you.
2. You can also add to any existing definitions.

**Reflection Questions**

| Produce | Purchase | Workshop Materials |
| --- | --- | --- |
| | | Laminated activity instructions. |
| | | Various color flipchart markers. |
| | | Wall or other hard surface. |
| | | Self-sticking flipchart paper or flipchart paper with an easel. |

| Topic Title | Learning Objective | |
| --- | --- | --- |

**Foundational Content**

| Activity Title | | Estimated Time |
| --- | --- | --- |
| (Postcards) | | 10 minutes |

**Activity Description**

Thirty numbered photo cards are spread out on the table in numerical order. Participants choose a blank index card, write the number of the photo that inspired them on it, and then describe on the index card how that photo relates to their understanding of the topic. They will then place their index card in a photo album–style binder for others to view.

| Learning Preference | | | | Interaction | | Technology |
| --- | --- | --- | --- | --- | --- | --- |
| ☐ Problem solving | ☐ Collaboration | ☐ Auditory | ☐ Reflective | ☒ Individual | ☐ Group | ☐ High tech |
| ☐ Competition | ☒ Visual | ☐ Kinesthetic | | ☐ Partner | ☐ Other | ☒ Low tech |

**Activity Instructions**

1. Choose a picture postcard that represents your view on the topic.
2. Take a blank index card and write the number on it from the postcard you chose.
3. Answer the following statement on your index card: "This image represents [the topic at hand] to me because . . ."
4. Place your index card in the binder for others to view.
5. Review your colleagues' postcards.

**Reflection Questions**

| Produce | Purchase | Workshop Materials |
| --- | --- | --- |
| | | Laminated activity instructions. |
| | | Table and chairs. |
| | | 30 4x6 photo cards, laminated. |
| | | 30 4x6 blank index cards for people to record their thoughts about the photos. |
| | | 8.5x11 binder with pages for 4x6 index cards. |

| Topic Title | Learning Objective |
| --- | --- |

## Foundational Content

| **Activity Title**<br>(Tic-Tac-Toe) | | **Estimated Time**<br>10 minutes |
| --- | --- | --- |

### Activity Description

Using dry-erase tic-tac-toe boards, learners partner up and take turns selecting true/false trivia cards. With each right answer, learners earn the right to place a mark ("X" or "O") on the board.

| **Learning Preference** | | | **Interaction** | **Technology** |
| --- | --- | --- | --- | --- |
| ☐ Problem solving | ☐ Collaboration | ☐ Auditory | ☐ Reflective | ☐ Individual | ☐ High tech |
| ☒ Competition | ☐ Visual | ☐ Kinesthetic | | ☒ Partner | ☒ Low tech |
| | | | | ☐ Group | |
| | | | | ☐ Other | |

### Activity Instructions

1. Decide who will go first. This learner is the "X", the second learner is the "O."
2. Select a card and read the true/false question aloud.
3. Answer the question and check your answer.
4. If you are correct place your mark (either "X" or "O") on the tic-tac-toe board.
5. Continue until you have either reached a stalemate or have a winner.

## Reflection Questions

| Produce | Purchase | **Workshop Materials** |
| --- | --- | --- |
| | | Laminated activity instructions. |
| | | Table. |
| | | Pre-made tic-tac-toe boards or create your own using a whiteboard and washi-style tape. |
| | | Two dry-erase markers. |
| | | 18 true/false questions on 5x7 cards, double-sided, laminated. Question on front; answer on back. |

| Topic Title | Learning Objective |
| --- | --- |

**Foundational Content**

| **Activity Title** (Timeline) | | **Estimated Time** 10 minutes |
| --- | --- | --- |

**Activity Description**

Learners place relevant events, processes, or milestones (related to the content) in chronological order on a timeline. Each event also includes a description highlighting its importance in the larger cultural context.

**Learning Preference**

| | | | **Interaction** | **Technology** |
| --- | --- | --- | --- | --- |
| ☐ Problem solving | ☐ Collaboration | ☐ Auditory | ☒ Individual | ☐ High tech |
| ☐ Competition | ☒ Visual | ☒ Kinesthetic | ☐ Partner | ☒ Low tech |
| | | ☐ Reflective | ☐ Group | |
| | | | ☐ Other | |

**Activity Instructions**

1. Read all the cards, but do not flip them over.
2. Organize all cards in the order in which you think the events happened.
3. When you think that the events are in the right order, flip each card over to find out if you're correct.

**Reflection Questions**

| Produce | Purchase | Workshop Materials |
| --- | --- | --- |
| | | Laminated activity instructions. |
| | | Table and chairs. |
| | | 10-15 double-sided laminated timeline cards, with the year on one side and the milestone (along with pop culture cues to help learners place the events) on the other. |
| | | Laminated timeline for learners to add the cards to. |

| Topic Title | Learning Objective |
|---|---|

**Foundational Content**

| Activity Title | Estimated Time |
|---|---|
| (Storytelling) | 10 minutes |

**Activity Description**

Using a recording device, learners record themselves telling a personal story in response to questions or cues related to the topic. The stories are also available for others to hear during the workshop.

| Learning Preference | | Interaction | | Technology | |
|---|---|---|---|---|---|
| ☐ Problem solving | ☐ Collaboration | ☒ Individual | ☐ Group | ☐ High tech | |
| ☐ Competition | ☒ Visual | ☐ Partner | ☐ Other | ☒ Low tech | |
| ☐ Auditory | ☒ Reflective | | | | |
| ☐ Kinesthetic | | | | | |

**Activity Instructions**

1. Select a story prompt.
2. Using the recording device, record yourself reading the story prompt and your response.
3. Stop recording when you're done.
4. Recorded stories will be available for others to view during the workshop.

**Reflection Questions**

| Produce | Purchase | Workshop Materials |
|---|---|---|
| | | Laminated activity instructions. |
| | | Recording device. |
| | | Two story prompts related to the topic of your workshop, printed. |

**Topic Title**
(Debrief)

**Learning Objective**

**Foundational Content**

**Activity Title**
(Debrief)

**Estimated Time**
10 minutes

**Activity Description**
As the facilitator, ask learners to share their takeaways and observations using notecards. You can have the questions prepared on each notecard, or you can ask them aloud to the group and ask the learners to write their response. Gather all notecards, and one at time, read a notecard response to share the learner's experience with the group.

**Learning Preference**

| | | | Interaction | Technology |
|---|---|---|---|---|
| ☐ Problem solving | ☐ Collaboration | ☐ Auditory | ☐ Individual | ☐ High tech |
| ☐ Competition | ☐ Visual | ☐ Kinesthetic | ☐ Partner | ☒ Low tech |
| | | ☒ Reflective | ☒ Group | |
| | | | ☐ Other | |

**Activity Instructions**
On your notecard, answer the following questions:

- How did this topic cause you to think differently about (topic)?
- What surprised you most about (topic)?
- What is one thing that inspired you today?
- What will you do differently as a result of your learning experience today?

**Reflection Questions**

| Produce | Purchase | Workshop Materials |
|---|---|---|
| | | Notecards, either blank or prepared with questions. |

# REFERENCES

Ahluwalia, R., and R.E. Burnkrant. 1993. "A Framework for Explaining Multiple Request Effectiveness: The Role of Attitude Towards the Request." *Advances in Consumer Research* 20: 620-624.

Bateson, P., and P. Martin. 2013. *Play, Playfulness, Creativity and Innovation.* Cambridge, UK: Cambridge University Press.

Bingham, T., and M. Conner. 2015. *The New Social Learning: Connect, Collaborate, Work.* Alexandria, VA: ATD Press.

Borzak, L., ed. 1981. *Field Study. A Source Book for Experiential Learning.* Beverly Hills, CA: Sage Publications.

Brown. S., and C. Vaughan. 2010. *Play: How It Shapes the Brain, Opens the Imagination, and Invigorates the Soul.* New York: Avery.

Burger, J.M. 1999. "The Foot-in-the-Door Compliance Procedure: A Multiple-Process Analysis and Review." *Personality and Social Psychology Review* 3: 303-325.

Bynum, W.F., and R. Porter, eds. 2005. *Oxford Dictionary of Scientific Quotations.* Oxford, UK: Oxford University Press.

Cain, S. 2012. *Quiet: The Power of Introverts in a World That Can't Stop Talking.* New York: Crown Publishers.

Carter, C., A. MacDonald, and S. Ursu. 2000. November. Based on Findings Presented at the 30th Annual Meeting of the Society for Neuroscience, New Orleans, LA.

CAST (Center for Applied Special Technology). 2011. *Universal Design for Learning Guidelines Version 2.0.* Wakefield, MA: CAST.

Collis, B., and A. Margaryan. 2004. "Applying Activity Theory to a Computer-Supported Collaborative Learning and Work-Based Activities in Corporate Settings." *Educational Technology Research and Development Journal* 52 (4): 38-52.

Cross, J. 2007. "What Is Informal Learning?" Informal Learning blog, November 27, 2007. www.informl.com/the-informal-learning-page.

Dewey, J. 1910. *How We Think*. Boston: D.C. Heath and Company.

Donston-Miller, D. 2012. "Why Your Business Can't Ignore Social Networking." *Networking Computing*, January 6. www.networkcomputing.com /networking/why-your-business-cant-ignore-social-networking/1104790041.

Dosher, B.A., and G. Rosedale. 1989. "Integrated Retrieval Cues as a Mechanism for Priming in Retrieval From Memory." *Journal of Experimental Psychology: General* 118 (2): 191-211.

Ernst, A., and J. Frisén. 2015. "Adult Neurogenesis in Humans—Common and Unique Traits in Mammals." *PLoS Biology* 13 (1): e1002045. http://doi .org/10.1371/journal.pbio.1002045.

Freedman, J.L., and S.C. Fraser. 1966. "Compliance Without Pressure: The Foot-in-the-Door Technique." *Journal of Personality and Social Psychology* 4 (2): 195-202.

Gallup. 2013. *State of the Global Workplace: Employee Engagement Insights for Business Leaders Worldwide*. Washington, D.C.: Gallup.

Geen, R.G. 1984. "Preferred Stimulation Levels in Introverts and Extroverts: Effects on Arousal and Performance." *Journal of Personality and Social Psychology* 46 (6): 1303-1312.

Hattie, J.A. 2009. *Visible Learning: A Synthesis of Over 800 Meta-Analyses Relating to Achievement*. London: Routledge.

Jensen, E. 2000. *Brain-Based Learning: The New Science of Teaching and Training*. San Diego, CA: The Brain Store Publishing.

Kolb, D. 1984. *Experiential Learning: Experience as the Source of Learning and Development*. Englewood Cliffs, NJ: Prentice Hall.

Lawson, C. 2002. "The Connections Between Emotions and Learning." The Center for Development & Learning blog, January 1. www.cdl.org/articles /the-connections-between-emotions-and-learning.

Li, M., W.H. Mobley, and A. Kelley 2013. "When Do Global Leaders Learn Best to Develop Cultural Intelligence? An Investigation of the Moderating Role of Experiential Learning Style." *Academy of Management Learning and Education* 12 (1): 32-50.

Looss, M. 2001. "Types of Learning?: A Pedagogic Hypothesis Put to the Test." Organisation for Economic Co-operation and Development, Paris. www.oecd .org/edu/ceri/34926352.pdf.

Marquardt, M. 2004. "Harnessing the Power of Action Learning." *T+D* 8 (6): 26-32.

Martin, A., and M. van Turennout. 2002. "Searching for the Neural Correlates of Object Priming." In *The Neuropsychology of Memory,* 3rd ed., edited by L.R. Squire and D.L. Schacter. New York: The Guilford Press.

Medina, J. 2008. *Brain Rules: 12 Principles for Surviving and Thriving at Work, Home, and School.* Seattle: Pear Press.

Monk, D. 2013. "John Dewey and Adult Learning in Museums." *Adult Learning* 24 (2): 63-71.

Montessori, M. 1946. *Education for a New World.* Madras, India: Kalakshetra Publications.

Nichols, M. 2006. "Great Employees Make a Great Business" Bloomberg, March 31. www.bloomberg.com/news/articles/2006-03-30/great-employees-make-a -great-business.

Park, A. 2014. "The Connection Between Play and Problem-Solving." *Chief Learning Officer*, October 2. www.clomedia.com/2014/10/02/the-connection -between-play-and-problem-solving.

Petty, G. n.d. "An Introduction to Constructivism." http://geoffpetty.com /for-teachers/active-learning.

Pink, D.H. 2009. *Drive: The Surprising Truth About What Motivates Us.* New York: Riverhead Books.

Prince, M. 2004. "Does Active Learning Work? A Review of the Research." *Journal of Engineering Education* 93 (3): 223-231.

Quinn, C.N. 2014. *Revolutionize Learning & Development: Performance and Innovation Strategy for the Information Age.* San Francisco: Wiley.

Ratcliff, R., and G. McKoon. 1988. "A Retrieval Theory of Priming in Memory." *Psychological Review* 95 (3): 385-408.

Rifkin, G. 2013. "What Do P. Diddy, Sergey Brin, and Peter Drucker Have in Common?" *Korn Ferry Briefings Magazine,* Q1.

Schwartz, B. 2004. *The Paradox of Choice: Why More Is Less.* New York: Harper Perennial.

Shaw, R.A. 2011. "Employing Universal Design for Instruction." *New Directions for Student Services* 134 (21): 22-23.

Shute, N. 2009. "10 Reasons Play Can Make You Healthy, Happy, and More Productive." *U.S. News & World Report*, March 9. http://health.usnews.com /health-news/family-health/childrens-health/articles/2009/03/09/10-reasons -play-can-make-you-healthy-happy-and-more-productive.

Ultanir, E. 2012. "An Epistemological Glance at the Constructivist Approach: Constructivist Learning in Dewey, Piaget, and Montessori." *International Journal of Instruction* 5 (2): 195-212.

Vail, P.L. 1994. *Emotion: The On/Off Switch of Learning.* Rosemont, NJ: Modern Learning Press.

Wesson, J. 2010. "Neuroplasticity." http://brainworldmagazine.com/neuroplasticity.

Wick, C.W., R.V.H. Pollock, A. Jefferson, and R. Flanagan. 2006. *The Six Disciplines of Breakthrough Learning: How to Turn Training and Development into Business Results,* 1st ed. San Francisco: Pfeiffer.

Wood, E.J. 1989. "Making Lectures More Exciting." *Biochemical Education* 17 (1): 9-12.

Zuckerman, M., J. Porac, D. Lathin, R. Smith, and E.L. Deci. 1978. "On the Importance of Self-determination for Intrinsically Motivated Behaviour." *Personality and Social Psychology Bulletin* 4: 443-446.

# ABOUT THE AUTHORS

Jillian Douglas and Shannon McKenzie, co-founders of Idea Learning Group in Portland, Oregon, have been on a mission to transform workplace learning by providing clients with creative, engaging, and custom learning experiences. Since its inception in 2009, Idea Learning Group has quickly grown into a well-known staple within the Pacific Northwest's learning and development community and was named one of Oregon's 100 fastest growing private companies by the *Portland Business Journal* in 2014, 2015, and 2016.

With more than 40 combined years of experience in adult learning, Shannon and Jillian's passion for improving how adults experience learning, along with their consistent work ethic and sharp-witted style, make them the perfect authors for *Let Them Choose: Cafeteria Learning Style for Adults.*

# INDEX

In this index, *f* denotes figure and *t* denotes table.

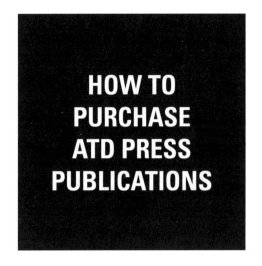

**HOW TO PURCHASE ATD PRESS PUBLICATIONS**

ATD Press publications are available worldwide in print and electronic format.

To place an order, please visit our online store: www.td.org/books.

Our publications are also available at select online and brick-and-mortar retailers.

Outside the United States, English-language ATD Press titles may be purchased through the following distributors:

**United Kingdom, Continental Europe, the Middle East, North Africa, Central Asia, Australia, New Zealand, and Latin America**
Eurospan Group
Phone: 44.1767.604.972
Fax: 44.1767.601.640
Email: eurospan@turpin-distribution.com
Website: www.eurospanbookstore.com

**Asia**
Cengage Learning Asia Pte. Ltd.
Phone: (65)6410-1200
Email: asia.info@cengage.com
Website: www.cengageasia.com

**Nigeria**
Paradise Bookshops
Phone: 08033075133
Email: paradisebookshops@gmail.com
Website: www.paradisebookshops.com

**South Africa**
Knowledge Resources
Phone: +27 (11) 706.6009
Fax: +27 (11) 706.1127
Email: sharon@knowres.co.za
Web: www.kr.co.za

For all other territories, customers may place their orders at the ATD online store: **www.td.org/books**.

0215145.62220